# Words of Hope

# Words of Hope

*Jesus Speaks Through the Saints*

**Edited by Craig Turner**

TAN Books
Charlotte, North Carolina

Cataloging-in-Publication data on file with the Library of Congress.

Typeset by Lapiz Digital Services.

Cover design by Caroline Kiser.

Cover image: Bloch, Carl (1834-90). *The Visitation*, oil on canvas, (Frederiksborg Castle, Hillerod, Denmark).

ISBN: 978-0-89555-717-9

Published in the United States by
TAN Books
P.O. Box 410487
Charlotte, NC 28241
www.TANBooks.com

Printed and Bound in the United States of America.

# A NOTE TO THE READER

The primary texts used in this book from which the locutions were taken include:

*The Spiritual Doctrine of St. Catherine of Genoa*, by Saint Catherine of Genoa and Don Cattaneo Marabotto. TAN Books, 1989. (CoG)

*The Autobiography of Saint Margaret Mary*, translated by the Sisters of the Visitation (Partridge Green, Horsham, West Sussex). TAN Books, 1986. (MMA)

*Saint Teresa of Avila, Collected Works, Vol. 1*, translated by Kieran Kavanaugh, O.C.D. and Otilio Rodriguez, O.C.D. ICS (Institute of Carmelite Studies) Publications, 1976. (TA)

*The Life and Revelations of St. Gertrude the Great* (Books I–V), by Saint Gertrude the Great and the Religious of her monastery. TAN Books, 2009. (GG)

Quotes were used as they appear in the original works with the exception of some modernization of the usage of words. For example, "thee" and "thy" were updated to read "you" and "your."

# ACKNOWLEDGMENTS

A NUMBER of different people deserve credit for their invaluable assistance in the production of this book. Among those are the people who gave time and effort without pay for compiling quotes from their sources and writing the biographies of their particular saints. These people include Fae Presley (Saint Teresa of Avila), Michael Seagriff (Saint Margaret Mary Alacoque), Tom Sherry (Saint Catherine of Genoa), and Laura Brestovansky (Saint Gertrude the Great).

Another source of inspiration and help was Bob French, who assisted in editing and gave recommendations when needed. I am also indebted to the staff at TAN Books, and to Todd Aglialoro in particular, for guidance and suggestions when difficult choices were necessary. Finally, I would like to thank the Blessed Virgin Mary for her prayers and assistance, sometimes felt and always appreciated, in helping bring this book to completion.

# CONTENTS

# INTRODUCTION

I WILL never forget the first time I heard that a person can hear the voice of God. In 1992, I was twenty-nine years old and in the midst of a major conversion experience that would lead me away from my strongly held atheistic convictions and into the Catholic Church. I had prided myself in my skills at debating and oratory, and had convinced some, perhaps many, that God was merely a figment of one's imagination. I was so unschooled in the topic of religion during those early months of my conversion that I didn't even know the meaning of the word "grace," and was taught its meaning while sitting in the office of a holy priest, the first Catholic cleric I would meet as an adult. As my conversion took hold during the fall of that year, a good friend introduced me to the life of Saint Francis of Assisi, the renowned stigmatist who gave up everything he owned—including the clothes on his back, which he returned to his father—to be closer to God.

The story about Saint Francis that moved me is one that has been retold many times. The story began when Francis traveled along a worn path in the Umbrian hills of Italy to pray at the church of San Damiano, a crumbling relic of stone and mortar. The church was so dilapidated and poor, that the only adornments in the building were an altar and a crucifix. While inside the church, kneeling before the large Byzantine crucifix, he distinctly heard the words, "Francis,

Francis, rebuild my church, for as you can see it is falling down." Three times the youthful Francis heard this sentence in his heart, and when he came to himself after this experience, he first gave back to his father all he owed him, and then returned to rebuild the little decrepit church of San Damiano, overgrown with brambles and weeds. It was a difficult but glorious undertaking that took months to complete. Francis worked by day and slept in the evening on the stone floor of the church with a tattered roof, peering out through the missing timbers at the starry Italian sky before finally dozing off to sleep. When his work at San Damiano was complete, he continued to rebuild, but this time he took on the massive structure of the Catholic Church, considerably larger in both size and complexity. He worked in this vineyard until he died: the founder of a new religious order, a worker of miracles, and a bearer of the stigmata, the wounds of Christ.

During his years as a laborer for Christ, he continued to hear the voice of his master, who guarded him from temptations and directed his soul toward holiness. In one inspiring episode, Francis was tempted to give up his hard labors, being shown a false image of what he would become if he did not cease his fasting, mortifications, and work:

> The ancient enemy strove to turn [Francis] away from his resolution, putting the image of a hunchback woman of Assisi in his mind, and warning him that if he did not abandon what he had undertaken, he would become like her. But Our Lord comforted him, and he heard the words, "Francis, put the bitter ahead of the sweet, and despise yourself, if you would know me."
>
> —The Golden Legend

What is astonishing about the locution Francis received is that Saint Bridget of Sweden, who lived more than a hundred years later, received a nearly identical locution from the Virgin Mary:

> "Which of the saints," Mary said, "had the sweetness of the Spirit without first experiencing bitterness? Therefore, one who craves sweetness must not flee from things that are bitter."
>
> —Life and Selected Revelations
> (Fifth Book, Fifth Interrogation)

Our Lord will repeat his messages through the centuries to those who dare to listen, and while speaking to his servants, will tell them either the exact message again, or a similar communication that reveals even more. Consider the following locution received by Saint Rose of Lima, the sixteenth-century hermit of South America who is Patroness of the Americas:

> Our Lord and Savior lifted up his voice and said with incomparable majesty, "Let all men know that without the burden of afflictions, it is impossible to reach the height of grace. Let them know that the gift of grace increases as the struggle increases."

Jesus' statement that one should not flee bitterness if one is to experience the sweetness of the Spirit becomes even more imperative: that to receive the gift of grace one must bear the burden of afflictions. For those who live lives of comfort, this statement can be a terrible thorn. But for those who suffer, the sweetness of these words can be the most succulent of nectars.

Our story, however, is not about these venerable examples of holiness—Francis of Assisi, Bridget of Sweden and Rose of Lima—but about saints whose lives were equally outstanding. In chronological order, they are: Saint Gertrude the Great (1256–1302), Saint Catherine of Genoa (1447–1510), Saint Teresa of Avila (1515–1582) and Saint Margaret Mary Alacoque (1647–1690).

These four saints received messages from Jesus that are of inestimable value to Christians seeking holiness. When the faithful meditate devoutly upon these locutions, and, with God's grace, apply the wisdom found therein to their daily lives, great fruit is sure to follow.

## Continuity of Messages

One of the most striking proofs of the validity of the messages that Jesus gives to the saints, touched on briefly above, is the continuity of these messages. Regardless of the time, place or culture the recipients live in, and notwithstanding their gender, level of education or social status, the revelations that Jesus gives to the saints never conflict with other messages or the Gospel. Saint Faustina, for example, lived during the twentieth century, but despite the fact that she was uneducated and had not read heavy theological works, was given messages by Jesus that are identical in content to those received by other saints throughout the ages.

Consider, for example, the topic of obedience. Josefa Menendez wrote about the messages she received regarding God's great love for obedience; obedience not only to God Himself, but also to those who are our superiors here on earth. When speaking about Jesus, Josefa asserted: "He showed me clearly that what pleases Him most is to do little acts out of obedience."[1]

Mary of the Trinity, a contemporary of Josefa Menendez, learned the exact same lesson despite the fact that the two did not know each other. The Master went so far as to tell Mary of the Trinity that obedience carries with it repercussions, not only for her, but for the entire Church and the world.

> My little daughter, the least act of obedience, because it is done in union with Me, the least fidelity of your holy rule [the vows taken as a nun], has its repercussions on the entire Church. Would you believe it? In the same way your failings, the smallest of your acts of cowardice, has its repercussion on the entire world— by its consequences. Would you believe it?[2]

Saint Margaret Mary, living 250 years before Josefa Menendez and Mary of the Trinity, also received messages regarding obedience, and she intoned that one becomes holy through obedience as well as poverty and chastity: "He now changed His manner toward me, making me see the beauty of virtue, especially of the three vows of poverty, chastity, and obedience, and telling me that by observing them one becomes holy."[3]

One of the most important observations we can make is to see that regardless of the culture or time period, Jesus repeats the same message to us. The following are Jesus'

---

1 Gottenmoller, Bartholomew, ed. *Words of Love: Revelations of Our Lord to Three Victim Souls in the 20th Century.* Charlotte: TAN Books, 2009.

2 Ibid.

3 *The Autobiography of St. Margaret Mary Alacoque.* Charlotte: TAN Books, 2009.

words to different people during different centuries regarding obedience:

# Thirteenth Century

"Whoever observes the regular [six-month] fast because of zeal for religious observance and purely for My love, and who seeks not his own advantage but Mine, I will accept it from him. . . . But if obedience and necessity obliges him to relax his fast against his will, and he submits in union with the humility with which I submitted to men when on earth for the glory of My Father, I will treat him as a friend would his dearest friend whom he had invited to his table." (GG)

# Sixteenth Century

Regarding the penance that another nun would undertake, Jesus said: "Do you see all the penance she does? I value your obedience more." (TA)

# Seventeenth Century

"But listen, believe not lightly and trust not every spirit, for Satan is enraged and will seek to deceive you. Therefore do nothing without the approval of those who guide you. Being thus under the authority of obedience, his efforts against you will be in vain, for he has no power over the obedient." (MMA)

"I am satisfied that you should prefer the will of your superiors to Mine whenever they may forbid you to do what I command you." (MMA)

"Therefore, not only do I desire that you should do what your superiors command, but also that you should do nothing at all that I order you without their consent. I love obedience, and without it no one can please me." (MMA)

## Twentieth Century

"Know this, that if I should ask one thing of you and your superiors another, I prefer you to obey them rather than me."[4]

"Every time you obey, you offer Me through visible actions the invisible love with which I fill your heart."[5]

"By obedience you give great glory to Me and gain merit for yourself."[6]

"My daughter, know that you give Me greater glory by a single act of obedience than by long prayers and mortifications."[7]

This final message, given to Saint Faustina during the twentieth century, is striking. Jesus indicates that long prayers and mortifications are of less value to Him than a single act of obedience. His statement does not mean that prayers and mortifications are of no value, because Jesus has spoken many

---

4 Josefa Menendez in *Words of Love: Revelations of Our Lord to Three Victim Souls in the 20th Century* edited by Gottenmoller, Bartholomew. Charlotte: TAN Books, 2009.

5 Mary of the Trinity in Ibid.

6 Saint Faustina in *Diary of St. Maria Faustina Kowalska: Divine Mercy in My Soul.* Stockbridge, Mass.: Marian Press, 1987.

7 Ibid.

times of the beauty and worth of even the smallest prayers and sacrifices. But consider that of even greater value than these is a small act done out of obedience.

Thus, the synthesis of these messages is that Jesus values obedience to an extraordinary degree, and that the faithful Christian must live an obedient life in order to please the Master. We read in Scripture the echo of this idea, because it is through Adam and Eve's disobedience that we contract a mortal blow we refer to as "original sin."

Before we move to the actual texts, it is important to consider briefly the lives of the saints who are the basis of this book, so that we might not only marvel at their gifts, but also attempt to imitate their lives.

# Saint Biographies

## St. Gertrude the Great (1256–1302)

Saint Gertrude is one of the few saints, and the only female saint, to be recognized by the Catholic Church with the appellation, "the Great." She is well-known and beloved for her many writings and extraordinary holiness. Her family entrusted her to the Benedictine convent at Helfta in Saxony (now part of Germany) when she was only five years old and she subsequently made her vows at fifteen. She was elected abbess of her Benedictine monastery in 1294. She ruled with charity and zeal and was well known as an excellent spiritual guide. Starting at age twenty-five, she was blessed with many visions of Jesus and Mary, many of which have been recounted in the 500-page autobiography *The Life and Revelations of St. Gertrude the Great.* She also wrote a book of spiritual exercises that still inspires many today. One of her closest friends also became a saint—Saint Mechtilde—and many of the anecdotes in that autobiography refer to their friendship.

Many of Saint Gertrude's prayers still inspire people today, particularly the following prayer, which Jesus told her would release a thousand souls from Purgatory each time it is said:

> O eternal Father, I offer you the Most Precious Blood of your divine son, Jesus, in union with the Masses said throughout the world today, for all the holy souls in Purgatory, for sinners everywhere, for sinners in the universal church, for those in my own home and within my family. Amen.

Saint Gertrude was also among the first people to be devoted to the Sacred Heart of Jesus, on which her love was centered some 400 years before that symbol was given more concisely to Saint Margaret Mary Alacoque. Saint Gertrude taught many people, through her teachings and her many writings, that God is merciful and wants each person to talk to him as they would a trusted friend, a novel concept during her lifetime. At that time, the more prevalent notion was of God as a stern and distant sovereign who was to be feared rather than loved.

One exceptional favor received by the saint is referred to as her "mystical marriage" to Jesus. After receiving many graces from Our Lord which she recounts in Chapter 21 of her book *Life and Revelations*, she told Jesus that He "had not assured me of these favors by solemn contract." To this Jesus replied, "Do not complain of this; approach and receive the confirmation of My promises." Jesus then opened both His hands and revealed His heart. Gertrude was told to extend her hand, and after receiving a gift, was told by Jesus that He would preserve the gifts He had given her. She said:

> After these most sweet words, as I withdrew my hand, I perceived seven golden circlets in the form of rings, one on each finger, and three on the signet finger, which indicated that the seven privileges were confirmed to me as I had asked.

This extraordinary favor is commemorated by the Church in Saint Gertrude's Office, which appears at the third antiphon at Lauds. It reads: "My Lord Jesus has espoused me to Him with seven rings, and crowned me as a bride."

Saint Gertrude died November 17, 1302 at the age of forty-six. Her feast day is November 16.

## St. Catherine of Genoa (1447–1510)

Located about seventy-five miles South of Milan, meandering along a narrow coastal plain adjacent to the western slopes of the Apennine Mountains, lies the historic and picturesque city of Genoa, Italy. The city's western edge shares the tranquil coastline of the Ligurian Sea in Italy's northwest, between Tuscany and the border of France.

It was here in 1447, four years before the birth of Christopher Columbus in this city, that Saint Catherine of Genoa (Caterina Fieschi Adorno), wife, widow and mystic, was born. The Renaissance also began in this region: Leonardo da Vinci was born about the same time (1452) in Florence, and Michelangelo was born in Tuscany only twenty-three years later.

A member of the nobility, Catherine's father, Jacopo Fieschi, enjoyed the esteemed position of Viceroy of Naples, which he held until his death. Her mother, Francesca di Negro, also of noble birth, was the daughter of Sigismund, Marquis di Negro.

As a child, Catherine demonstrated extraordinary holiness and love of God. Even as a little girl, we are told, she earnestly dedicated herself to lengthy prayer, meditation and penance, and she was well known for her deep and single-minded love of Jesus' passion.

When she was about thirteen years of age, Catherine made known her wishes to enter a convent and dedicate her life as a religious nun. She was understandably rejected at the time, however, because of her tender years. Ever obedient and resigned to her parents and to Church authority, she did not persist in pushing her personal desires. In fact, three years later she dutifully was given in marriage to a young Genoese man, also of noble birth, Giuliano Adorno. As was the custom, Giuliano had been chosen for Catherine in a prearranged union.

It would be nice to relate that Catherine rode off into the sunset and lived happily ever after, but it was, unfortunately, not to be so. Catherine's marriage was disastrous. Giuliano had a violent temper, spent their money mindlessly and was persistently unfaithful to her. True to her nature, Catherine silently and stoically endured Giuliano's constant abuse for the first five years of their marriage. Although he was of a noble family, he conducted their personal and financial affairs so poorly that the couple was reduced to abject poverty.

Showing early signs of a "saintly" disposition, Catherine was always obedient and patient with Giuliano's whims and eccentricities. At the same time, however, she suffered so much from his mercurial emotions that she was barely able to preserve her health and sanity. She finally became so exhausted and emaciated that she was as a living ghost, almost a walking object of pity.

For the first five years of her marriage Catherine lived alone and miserable most of the time because of her husband's prolonged, wanton absences. Attempting to keep the peace and to avoid his tantrums, she never left their residence except to attend Mass. Afterwards she would rush home as quickly as possible in order to avoid upsetting Giuliano.

Catherine endured this wretched lifestyle for as long as she could, and then decided she yearned for something better than the life of an unhappy recluse. For roughly the next five years she sought comfort and solace through innocent worldly distractions, hoping to take her mind off her marital problems and her enforced loneliness. She associated with other young ladies and tried to occupy herself with worldly affairs as they did.

No happier after these five years of aimless living, and by now trapped in a bad marriage for ten years, Catherine felt completely lost. With only a lukewarm love for God by this time, she began praying in earnest for the return of her religious zeal, her love of Christ's Passion and the strength to resume the penitential regimen she practiced as a young girl. Soon afterward she abandoned her "wandering" way of life for good. She began living with her husband in complete continence rather than as a married couple. Yet any semblance of peace or happiness still eluded her.

Catherine had been overwhelmed with mental suffering during this time and grew to despise everything connected with the world. She shunned the company of other people and suffered from such a deep depression that it kept her from taking part in any events or activities.

Her sister, a nun, became increasingly concerned about Catherine's state of mind, and finally insisted that she go to confession at her convent since their confessor was regarded as a holy man. Catherine's sister added that if the confessor couldn't help her, at least she would receive his blessing. Very reluctantly, but realizing that she needed the help, Catherine agreed.

This difficult decision ushered in a life-changing experience for Catherine, and a true miracle. After arriving at the convent she knelt in the confessional to give her confession, but was suddenly wounded with what could only be described as "the immensity of the love of God." The experience so overwhelmed her that she lost consciousness and fell into a mystical trance.

During the confession but just before she fell into her mystical trance, the confessor was providentially called away from the confessional for a few moments to attend to another matter. By the time he returned to hear Catherine's confession, she had no ability to speak clearly—she could only mumble that she needed to put off her confession until a later time. She immediately exited the confessional and returned home.

From the moment of her mystical illumination, Saint Catherine's interior life and relationship with God were radically changed, and would remain so for the rest of her life. While still alive, she was given the grace and realization of being placed mystically in the "Purgatory" of God's burning love, in whose flames she was purified from every stain of sin. She would fast each Advent and Lent for thirty and forty days, subsisting on only water mixed with vinegar or salt. Remarkably, her associates noticed no change in demeanor or energy from the saint during this time.

After her miraculous experience in the confessional, not much is recorded about her exterior life. But we do know that Catherine's husband, Giuliano, experienced his own conversion at a later time and became a member of the Third Order of Saint Francis. He subsequently incurred a fatal illness which took his life.

As Giuliano's end drew near, Catherine withdrew to a private place to pray intensely for him. There she cried and begged Jesus for the conversion of her husband. "O Love, I beg of you this soul. I pray, give it to me, for you can do it." She persisted intensely for thirty minutes praying in this manner, and then heard Our Lord interiorly say to her that her prayer had been answered. She returned to her husband's chamber to find him so calm and changed that, by every word and act, he was a different man. He died a holy death in 1497.

After the death of Giuliano until her own death, Catherine devoted herself uninterruptedly to the care of the sick in Genoa's hospital. She spent so much time there and was so proficient in her work that she eventually became manager and treasurer of the hospital. But the heavy labors and the burden of running the hospital took its toll on her health, and she died nearly exhausted in 1510. Upon opening her casket years later, witnesses found her body incorrupt, showing no signs of decay.

Saint Catherine is the source of three celebrated works: *Dialogues of the Soul and Body*, and two uniquely insightful works entitled *The Life and Doctrine of Saint Catherine of Genoa*, and *Treatise on Purgatory*.

## St. Teresa of Avila (1515–1582)

Born under the Catholic monarchy of Ferdinand and Isabella during the sixteenth century when Spain's dominance in the world was at its zenith, Saint Teresa of Avila became one of the greatest mystics of the Faith. A pious child but worldly teenager, Teresa nevertheless heard God's call and ran away from her father's house to enter the Carmelite monastery of the Incarnation. Teresa's spiritual experiences began as she immersed herself in prayer. While Teresa received little guidance in prayer from her monastery other than the Divine Office, a book entitled *Third Spiritual Alphabet* by the Franciscan Osuna propelled her forward into a life of interior, or mental, prayer. This prayer she saw as "an intimate sharing between friends . . . taking time frequently to be alone with Him who we know loves us."

The friendship between God and Teresa developed to such a degree that she often heard His voice and was totally enraptured by His presence, unaware of her surroundings and unable to move. A magnificent Renaissance sculpture by Bernini called *The Ecstasy of St. Teresa* sprang from her account in Chapter 29 of her autobiography of one of the most remarkable raptures of unity she experienced during her lifetime:

I saw an angel, very near me toward my left side, in
bodily form. . . . His face was so shining that he seemed
to be one of those highest angels called seraphs, who
look as if all on fire with divine love. I saw in his hand a
long spear of gold, and at the iron's point there seemed
to be a little fire. He appeared to me to be thrusting it
at times into my heart, and to pierce my very entrails.
When he drew it out, he seemed to draw them out
also, and to leave me all on fire with a great love of
God. The pain was so great that it made me moan,
and yet so surpassing was the sweetness of this exces-
sive pain that I could not wish to be rid of it. The soul
is satisfied now with nothing less than God.

Teresa's superiors ordered her to write an account of her life,
in which she describes many of her mystical experiences. She
was seen at times levitating while in prayer, produced a mul-
tiplication of wine for forty workers at a construction project,
was transfigured with a face "shining resplendently" on more
than one occasion, and was accompanied at times by a heavenly scent so strong that, after she died, the doors and win-
dows of the building had to be opened because the aroma was
so overpowering. Like Saint Catherine of Genoa, her body
did not decay after death.

Though afflicted with severe mysterious illnesses throughout her life, Teresa's apostolic activity was intense. Her apos-
tolate was a perfect blend of contemplation and action that
brought rich fruit to the life of the Carmelite Order, to the
Church and to the world. Desiring to restore the Carmelite
Order to its original state by minimizing all the comforts
and social pleasures that had crept into the Order over the
years (such as fancy meals, social time with outsiders and a

less-than-rigorous prayer life), Teresa founded a new house in Avila designed to be more austere. She was severely opposed. However, God Himself directed her work and the monastery of Saint Joseph was founded in 1562 for prayer, asceticism and austerity.

With the exception of five peaceful years Teresa spent with her sisters at Saint Joseph's and three years as prioress of the Monastery of the Incarnation, Teresa responded to the call of God to found house after house throughout Spain with toil and hardship. In twenty years she founded sixteen reformed Carmelite monasteries for nuns (today referred to as convents) and had a hand in founding numerous houses for friars. Teresa was a tireless traveler and endured great physical duress on these trips.

Teresa's final foundation was in Burgos, northern Spain, in April of 1582. Weary and extremely ill after this last foundation, she traveled to Alba de Tormes to visit a friend, stopping along the way at her Carmelite houses. She was not greeted warmly and endured hostility from the prioresses until at last she arrived in early October at Alba de Tormes. Taking to bed, she received the Last Rites and died in the arms of her faithful companion, exclaiming, "O my Lord, now is the time that we shall see each other!"

It is difficult to exaggerate the greatness of this saint, who was canonized in 1622, forty years after her death, and proclaimed a Doctor of the Church in 1970. She made full use of the gifts that God had given her: strength and courage against great odds, true humility in relying totally on God's grace, intelligence, boldness and obedience. Teresa's deep prayer life allowed her to become one of the Church's greatest teachers; it also was the foundation of her apostolic activity in reforming the Carmelite order and founding numerous convents across Spain and Portugal. Above all, her life witnessed to the greatness of God, not only of His power, but of His love.

## St. Margaret Mary Alacoque (1647–1690)

Saint Margaret Mary Alacoque was born on July 22, 1647 in Lhautecur, France, the fifth of seven children. At age four, without knowing its meaning, she found herself continually saying: "O my God, I consecrate to You my purity, and I make You a vow of perpetual chastity." Not surprisingly, Our Lord gave her such "an awareness of the hideousness of sin" that for her "the least stain was insupportable torment." Young Margaret also developed a great devotion to the Blessed Mother, who once, however, reprimanded her as she was reciting the rosary while seated in a chair with these words: "I am surprised, my daughter, that you serve me so negligently."

At age eight, six months after her father died, Margaret went to a convent school, and remained there for two years, the only formal education she would receive. She made her first Holy Communion there at nine years of age but had to leave because of illness. Margaret determined then to become a nun if she was cured.

Margaret and her ill mother were forced to live under the total control of three relatives. Neither of them had "any power in the house and dared not do anything without permission," she wrote later. It was as if they were captive slaves in their own home. Margaret accepted this trying situation, seeking strength and consolation from the Blessed Sacrament. Unfortunately, she was often denied permission to go to church.

Although Margaret was cured shortly after leaving the convent school, she struggled until age twenty-three with the conflicting desire to become a religious and her mother's plea to marry and take care of her. This caused her great torment and she frequently vacillated between these two desires. Throughout most of her life, she also fought two constant fears: sinning and being deceived.

She eventually chose to enter the convent but refused to join the Ursulines where friends and family expected her to go. She instead joined the Visitation nuns at Paray-le-Monial, a community founded by St. Francis de Sales. This was a religious order where none of the sisters were expected to seek, desire, or manifest any extraordinary spiritual gifts. Margaret sought not to bring any attention to herself, but the spiritual gifts and struggles and physical ailments God had given her were of such a nature that many of her fellow religious thought that she was possessed.

Margaret constantly struggled between doing what she felt God was prompting her to do and what her superiors directed her to do. The two directions often conflicted and caused her great spiritual torment and uncertainty. Eventually, the Lord told her to obey her superiors and to trust Him. She followed that advice, although at times it was very difficult for her to do so.

Our Lord once told her how greatly He loved men, even those from whom He received only ingratitude and contempt, telling her:

> I feel this more than all that I suffered during My passion. If only they would make Me some return for My love, I should think but little of all I have done for them and would wish, were it possible, to suffer still more. But the sole return they make for all My eagerness to do them good is to reject Me and treat Me with coldness.

Margaret agreed to console Him and make reparation on behalf of those who had rejected His love by receiving Holy Communion as often as obedience permitted it, by receiving Communion on the First Friday of each month, and by praying and reflecting on His passion every Thursday evening from eleven p.m. to midnight.

During another revelation, Our Lord showed Margaret His Sacred Heart for the first time and told her:

> My Divine Heart is so inflamed with love for men, and for you in particular that, being unable any longer to contain within itself the flames of its burning charity, it must spread them abroad by your means, and manifest itself to [mankind] in order to enrich them with the precious treasures which I [reveal] to you, and which contain graces of sanctification and salvation necessary to withdraw them from the abyss of perdition.

In 1674, after allowing Margaret to repose on His Sacred Heart, Our Lord asked for her heart, placed it in His and returning it called her "the beloved disciple of My Sacred

Heart." About one year later (June 16, 1675), Our Lord again appeared with His Sacred Heart exposed, telling Margaret:

> Behold this heart, which has loved men so much, that it has spared nothing, even to exhausting and consuming itself in order to testify to them its love; and in return I receive from the greater number nothing but ingratitude by reason of their irreverence and sacrileges, and by the coldness and contempt which they show Me in this sacrament of love. But what I feel the most keenly is that it is hearts which are consecrated to Me, that treat Me thus.

He then asked for the First Friday devotion to be established, requesting that the Friday after the Octave of Corpus Christi:

> Be set apart for a special feast to honor My heart, by communicating on that day and making reparation to it by a solemn act, in order to make amends for the indignities which it has received during the time it has been exposed on the altars. I promise you that My heart shall expand itself to shed upon those who shall thus honor it, and cause it to be honored.

Our Lord told Margaret to share this direction with her confessor, Saint Claude de la Colombiere, S.J., and assured her that this saintly priest would help her implement His plans. Eventually, through various signs from God, her superiors came to see that Margaret was in fact being led by Jesus and assisted her in founding the special devotions He had asked her to establish. The Church first celebrated this special feast day on August 31, 1670.

A subsequent confessor of Margaret, Father John Croiset, S.J., also helped promote this devotion through a book (recently reprinted) entitled *Devotion to the Sacred Heart*. In it, he sets forth a number of promises made by Our Lord for those who practice devotion to His Sacred Heart, including a way to bring profound graces to even the most obdurate souls, a method to obtain peace and harmony amongst people, and one of the greatest methods to conquer even the strongest passions and vices.

Saint Margaret Mary died on October 17, 1690. She was beatified in 1824 and canonized in 1920.

# Words of Hope

# Abandonment to God's Will

"My goodness is such that when anyone has the will to perform a good action, I count it as done and recompense it as if it were accomplished, even if human frailty prevents its accomplishment." (GG)

"I require nothing from you but to come to Me empty, that I may fill you, for it is from Me that you receive all which makes you agreeable in My sight." (GG)

"What bride would complain of the time spent adorning herself for her bridegroom, or regret occasions of increasing his love? For after death the soul cannot [gain] merit, nor can it suffer anything for God." (GG)

*Saint Margaret Mary prayed that Our Lord would never let anyone see what she had written in her journal about her spiritual experiences. He responded:* "Abandon everything to My good pleasure and let Me accomplish My designs. Do not interfere in anything, for I will take care of it all." (MMA)

*As Saint Gertrude prayed for someone, that he might receive the full reward of his troublesome labors for the temporal good of the community. Our Lord said to her:* "His will is so entirely submitted to Mine that I am always the principle cause of his actions, and for this reason he will merit an inestimable recompense for all his thoughts, his words and his works. If he applies himself to each action with a still greater purity of intention, he will increase his merit even as gold exceeds silver in value. If he endeavors to refer all his thoughts and anxieties to Me with a yet purer intention, they will become as much more excellent as refined gold is in comparison of that which is allowed with a baser metal." (GG)

"Even as the body is composed of many members united together, so also the soul consists of affections, such as fear, grief, joy, love, hope, anger, modesty, [etc]. In the exercise of each, the more [a] man acts for My glory, the more he will find in Me that incomprehensible and ineffable joy, and that secure delight, which will prepare him for eternal happiness." (GG)

*Jesus said:* "When a bridegroom conducts his bride into a garden of roses to gather them for a bouquet, she takes so much pleasure in his sweet conversation that she never pauses to inquire which of the roses he would wish her to gather, but she takes whatever flower her bridegroom gives her and places it in her bouquet. So also the faithful soul, whose greatest pleasure is the accomplishment of My will and [who] delights in it as in a garden of roses, is indifferent whether I restore her health or take her out of the present life, because, being full of confidence, she abandons herself entirely to My paternal care." (GG)

"He who is constantly suffering and still conforms himself to the decrees of Providence offers Me gold enriched with very rare and precious stones." (GG)

"I am the only true Friend who in dire necessity will console the afflicted with the merit and glory of all the good works they have practiced during their whole life, whether by thoughts, words, or actions. These shall appear scattered over My vestments like roses and lilies; while this delightful vision shall revive in the soul its hopes of eternal life, to which it beholds itself invited in recompense for its good works." (GG)

*Saint Gertrude prayed for someone who said she did not seem to receive any fruit from her prayers. The Lord told her:* "Let her confide in My wisdom and My divine mercy, since I am her father, her brother and her spouse, and I will obtain what will be advantageous for her body and soul with far more care and fidelity than she would for any relative. I will preserve carefully the fruit of all the prayers and desires which are addressed to Me for her until a suitable time comes to permit her to the enjoyment of them; then I will commit them to her entirely when no one will be able to corrupt them or to deprive her of them by their importunities. This is far more useful to her than to pour into her soul some sweetness which might, perhaps, be an occasion of vainglory to her or become tarnished by her pride, or than to grant her some temporal prosperity which might prove an occasion of sin." (GG)

"When anyone has lost, or fears to lose [by death] a faithful friend, if they offer Me this affliction and would rather My will should be accomplished than their friend should live, they may be assured if they form this desire in their hearts even for a single hour that I will preserve their offering in the same beauty and freshness as it was presented to Me. All those griefs and inquietudes which overwhelm man through the weakness of his human nature will only serve to make place in their souls for divine consolations after the offering of which I have spoken. I will bestow on them as many consolations as they have suffered afflictions. There is nothing which can be renounced in this life, however great,

which will not be restored a hundredfold in this life and a
thousandfold in eternity." (GG)

"If anyone desires, for love of Me, to undertake any painful work by which he fears to be hindered from his devotions,
if he prefers the accomplishment of My will to his soul's good,
I will so esteem the purity of his intention as to consider it as
if it had really been carried into action. Even if he never com-
mences what he has undertaken, he will not fail to obtain the
same reward from Me as if he had accomplished it and had
never committed the least negligence in the matter." (GG)

"If you desire that I should act as I will with you, give
Me the key of your heart, that I may leave or take away what-
ever I please." "And what is this key?" *inquired Saint Gertrude.*
*[Jesus] answered:* "It is your will." (GG)

*Once, Our Lord said to Saint Gertrude:* "If I granted you at
the moment of your death the accomplishment of all the holy
desires which you have entertained, it would be little in comparison with the grace I am about to confer on you. Choose
whether you will die now or suffer a long sickness first, that
you may know something of the infirmities of a protracted illness. *The saint replied:* "Lord, do Your holy will." *He answered:*
"You do right to submit to My decision, and if you consent,
for My love, to remain longer in the body, I will establish My
abode in your heart as a dove in its nest; and at the same time
I will hide you in My Heart from whence I will lead you forth
to eternal joys." (GG)

*After resolving to die rather than again abandon her desire
for a religious life, Saint Margaret Mary heard her divine spouse
ask her,* "whether, considering my weakness, I would agree to

His taking possession and making Himself master of my liberty. I willingly consented, and from that time forth He took such firm hold of my liberty that I never more enjoyed the use of it." *At a later date, Jesus told her,* "I will make you understand hereafter that I am a wise and learned director, who knows how to lead souls safely when they abandon themselves to Me and forget themselves." (MMA)

*Jesus said to Saint Margaret Mary:* "Let Me do everything in its time. For I will have you now to be the sport of My love, treating you according to its good pleasure, as children treat their play things. You must, therefore, abandon yourself blindly and without resistance, allowing Me to please Myself at your expense. You will lose nothing thereby. . . . Be ever ready and disposed to receive Me, for henceforth, I will make My abode in you that I may be able to hold familiar converse with you." (MMA)

*Saint Margaret Mary wrote:* "Moreover, He willed that I should receive everything as coming from Him without procuring anything for myself; that I should abandon all to Him without disposing of anything . . . that I should thank Him for suffering as well as for enjoyment . . . that on the most painful and humiliating occasions I should consider that I not only deserve these, but even greater ones . . . that I should offer the pain I experienced for the persons who afflicted me . . . that I was always to speak of Him with great respect, of my neighbor with esteem and compassion, and of myself never, or, at least, briefly and with contempt, unless for His glory He should make Me do otherwise . . . that I was ever to attribute all the good and the glory to His sovereign greatness, and all the evil to myself; never to seek consolation out of Him, and even when He granted it to me, to renounce and offer it to

Him. I was to cling to nothing, to empty and despoil myself of everything, to love nothing but Him, in Him and for the love of Him, and to see in all things nothing but Him and the interests of His glory in complete forgetfulness of myself." (MMA)

*After making her annual confession, Saint Margaret Mary seemed to see and to feel herself stripped and, at the same time, clothed with a white robe, while hearing these words:* "Behold the robe of innocence with which I clothe your soul, that you may henceforth live only the life of a man-God—that is to say, that you may live as no longer living, but allow Me to live in you—for I am your life, and you shall no longer live but in Me and by Me. My will is that you should act as no longer acting, leaving Me to act and work in you and for you, and abandoning all to My care. You must henceforth have no will, letting Me will for you in everything and everywhere as though you had none." (MMA)

*After Jesus had said this, she wrote that He continued His discourse by saying:* "'O children of the earth! How long will you be hard of heart?'" (MMA)

*Jesus said [to Saint Teresa] that* "I should examine one thing in myself: whether I was totally surrendered to Him or not [and] that if I was, I should believe He would not let me go astray." (TA) *Once, when Saint Teresa was anxiously desiring to help her order, the Carmelites, Jesus said to her:* "Do what lies in your power. Surrender yourself to Me and do not be disturbed about anything. Rejoice in the good that has been given you, for it is very great. My Father takes His delight in you and the Holy Spirit loves you." (TA)

"On the feast of the Presentation while praying to God very intensely for a person, it seemed to me it was still unbecoming the great sanctity I desired for this person that he have his freedom and an income. I considered his poor health and the abundant light he gave to souls, and I heard: 'He serves Me very much, but it is a great thing to follow Me stripped of everything as I was on the cross. Tell him to trust in Me.'" (TA)

"I find in him nothing which is contrary to Me but the free will which I have given him, and this I am always combating through love until he yields it to Me. And when I have accepted it I reform it little by little by My secret operations and loving care, and never abandon him until I have conducted him to his appointed end." (CoG)

## Answered Prayer

*Teresa of Avila wrote:* "Once while I was imploring the Lord to give sight to a person to whom I was obligated and who had almost completely lost his vision, I was very grieved and feared that because of my sins the Lord would not hear me. The Lord appeared to me as He did at other times and began to show me the wound in His left hand, and with the other hand He drew out a large nail that had been embedded there. It seemed to me that when the nail was pulled out, His flesh was torn out along with it. The sharp pain was clearly evident, and I felt great pity [for Him]. He told me that He who had suffered that for me should not be doubted, but that in a better way He would do what I had asked Him; that He had promised me there wasn't anything I might ask Him that He wouldn't do; that He already knew I wouldn't ask for anything other than what was in conformity with His glory; and that thus He would do what I was now requesting; that I should consider that even when I wasn't serving Him there wasn't anything I asked for that He didn't grant, and in a better way than I knew how to ask for; that how much more He would grant my petitions now that He knew I loved Him; and that I shouldn't doubt this. I don't think eight days passed before the Lord gave sight back to that person." (TA)

"Once I [Teresa of Avila] felt severely troubled because I knew that a person to whom I was very much obligated desired to do something serious against the honor of God, as well as his own. He was already very determined about the matter. My anxiety was so great I didn't know what to do. It no longer seemed there was any remedy to make him give up the idea. I begged the Lord with all my heart to provide a cure for him, but until seeing this cure I wasn't able to find any alleviation in my affliction. Being in such a state, I went to a secluded hermitage (for we have them in this monastery), and while in the one with the painting of Christ at the pillar, and begging Him to grant me this favor, I heard a very gentle voice speaking to me in a kind of whistling sound. My hair stood on end, for the voice frightened me. I wanted to understand what it was saying, but I couldn't because it passed very quickly. When my fear was gone, for it went away quickly, I felt such quiet and joy and interior delight that I marveled that just hearing the sound of a voice could effect so much in the soul. For I heard it with my bodily ears and without understanding a word. In this experience I realized that what I had asked for would be accomplished. As a result it happened that my affliction left me completely even though the prayer was not yet answered. The pain went away just as it would had I seen the prayer answered as it really was afterward." (TA)

"I [Teresa of Avila] knew a person who had resolved to serve God very earnestly and had devoted some days to prayer in which His majesty granted him many favors. Because of some occasions of sin that he was in, he gave up prayer and did not withdraw from these occasions, and they were indeed dangerous. This pained me deeply since he was a person I loved very much and to whom I owed a great deal. I believe it was more than a month in which I didn't do anything else but beg God to bring this soul back to Himself. One day, while in prayer, I saw a devil at my side who very angrily was tearing to shreds some papers he had in his hands. This gave me great consolation, for it seemed to me that what I had been asking for had been accomplished. And so it was, for afterward I learned that this person had made his confession with great contrition and returned to God so sincerely that I hope . . . he will always make progress. May God be blessed forever. Amen." (TA)

"It often happens that Our Lord draws souls away from serious sin and also that He leads others to greater perfection because of my beseeching Him. The Lord has granted me so many favors by freeing souls from Purgatory and doing other noteworthy things, that I would tire myself and tire whoever reads this if I mentioned them all. He has granted much more in regard to the health of souls than He has in regard to the health of bodies." (TA)

## Charity

"Charity not only covers sins, but, like a burning sun, consumes and annihilates the slightest imperfections and overwhelms the soul with merit." (GG)

"She who wearies herself in exercises of charity has a right to repose peacefully on the couch of charity." (GG)

"Toward persons who spoke evil of me, not only did I feel I bore no harsh feelings, but it seemed to me I gained a new love for them. I don't know how this came about. It was a blessing given by the hand of the Lord." (TA)

". . . It seemed to me I knew clearly in an intellectual vision that the entire Blessed Trinity was present. In this state my soul understood by a certain kind of representation (like an illustration of the truth), in such a way that my dullness could perceive, how God is three and one. And so it seemed that all three Persons were represented distinctly in my soul and that they spoke to me, telling me that from this day I would see an improvement in myself in respect to three things and that each one of these Persons would grant me a favor: one, the favor of charity; another, the favor of being able to suffer gladly; and the third, the favor of experiencing this charity with an enkindling in the soul. I understood those words the Lord spoke [and] that the three divine Persons would be with the soul in grace, for I saw them within myself in the way described." (TA)

## Chosen Souls

"You cannot find Me in any place in which I delight more or which is more suitable for Me than in the Sacrament of the Altar, and after that, in the heart and soul of Gertrude, My beloved; for towards her all My affections turn in a singular manner." (GG)

"Come to Me, because I love you and desire that you should be always present before Me as My beloved spouse. Therefore I call you, and because My delights are in you, I desire that you should enter into Me. Furthermore, because I am the God of love, I desire that you should remain indissolubly united to Me, even as the body is united to the spirit, without which it cannot live for a moment." (GG)

*Saint Gertrude was troubled that someone for whom she had cared for deeply seemed to treat her efforts with contempt. The Lord told her:* "Do not be grieved, My daughter, for I have permitted this to happen for your eternal welfare, that I may the oftener enjoy your company and conversation, in which I take so much pleasure. Desiring to have you always near Me, I permit your friends to contradict you in some things, that you may find no true fidelity in any creature and therefore have recourse to Me with all the more eagerness, because you know that I possess the plenitude and stability of all contentment." (GG)

*Jesus Christ once appeared to Saint Gertrude, and showing her His Heart, said to her:* "My beloved, give Me your heart." *She presented it to Him with profound respect. It seemed to her that He united it to His by a canal which reached to the ground, through which He poured forth abundantly the effusions of His infinite grace, saying to her:* "Henceforth I shall use your heart as a canal through which I shall pour forth the impetuous torrents of mercy and consolation which flow from My loving Heart on all those who shall dispose themselves to receive it by having recourse to you with humility and confidence." (GG)

*In studying the life of Saint Augustine, Saint Gertrude asked,* "O Lord, how can he be so pure when he must have contracted so many stains in his wanderings from the faith before his conversion?" *Jesus replied:* "I permitted these wanderings, awaiting his return with patience and mercy and then overwhelming him with My gratuitous favors." *Then, comparing Saint Augustine to Saint Bernard, Saint Gertrude asked,* "My Lord, was not Saint Bernard as devoted to you as Saint Augustine, whose glory shines so resplendently? Yet it seems to me that he does not enjoy the same delights." *Our Lord replied:* "Bernard, My chosen one, has received an immense recompense, but your mind is not capable of discerning the glory of even the least of My saints. How then, can it discern that of the greatest? Nevertheless, to satisfy your devotion, to increase your love and that you may know how many mansions there are in My Father's house, understand this: Though all the saints possess [God's] glory, they do not possess it in the same degree, but each according to their merit." (GG)

*As one of the sisters lay dying, St. Gertrude prayed for her with others, and said to the Lord,* "Why don't you hear our prayers for her, O most loving Lord?" *Jesus replied:* "Her soul is in such a different state from the souls of others that she cannot be consoled by you in a human manner. My majesty will enthrone itself in her. She will be absorbed in My divinity, as a sunbeam absorbs a drop of dew." (GG)

"Gertrude is a spiritual ark. I desire that she should contain manna—that is to say, the sweetness and tenderness of charity to console the souls under her guidance and to solace their grief as far as she can. I desire also that she should possess the Tablets of the Law—that is to say that she should declare or forbid what should be done or not done in order to please

Me, and that in so doing she should be guided by the lights and discernment with which I have enlightened her. But I desire also that she should be the rod of Aaron—that is to say, the authority and zeal of justice, to correct those persons who stray from their duty, to prescribe and impose salutary penances, and to decide and regulate everything with a fervent and even mind. She should consider that I could easily reform what needs reform or what is ill-regulated, by simple inspirations or by trials and disgraces, but I effect these things through her to increase her merit. And if anyone fails to profit by her warnings and corrections, it shall be no prejudice to Gertrude since she has done her duty and has employed all the care and vigilance possible to convert the sinner: Man may plant and water, but I only can give the increase." (Cf. 1 Cor. 3:6) (GG)

"I have chosen you to be My spouse, and we pledged each other fidelity when you made your vow of chastity. It was I who urged you to make it, before the world had any share in your heart, because I wished to have it quite pure and unsullied by any worldly affections. And in order to preserve it thus, I removed all malice from your will so that it should not be corrupted . . . I then confided you to the care of My holy Mother, that she might fashion you according to My designs." (MMA)

*Saint Margaret Mary pleaded with Jesus to allow her to live an ordinary religious life and not one manifested by extraordinary graces. Jesus replied:* "Let us continue the conflict, My daughter. I am quite content to do so. We will see who will be victorious, the creator or His creature, strength or weakness, the all-powerful or powerlessness. But whoever is conqueror will remain so forever." (MMA)

*Saint Margaret Mary:* "He likewise forbade me to judge, accuse, or condemn anyone but myself. . . . He told me to fear nothing, for He was a good master, being as powerful to have His teaching carried into effect as He was all-wise both to teach and to govern well. Thus I can affirm that, whether I would or not, I was obliged to do what He wished in spite of my natural repugnance." (MMA)

*At a Mass honoring Saint Benedict, Saint Gertrude prayed to know what special rewards he had received. Saint Benedict answered:* "All who invoke me, remembering the glorious end which God honored me, shall be assisted by me at their death with such fidelity that I will place myself where I see the enemy most disposed to attack them. Thus fortified by My presence, they will escape the snares which he lays for them and depart happily and peacefully to the enjoyment of eternal beatitude." (GG)

"Once," *wrote Teresa of Avila about a jeweled crucifix she was given by Jesus,* "when I was holding in my hand the cross of a rosary, He put out His own hand and took it from me, and, when He gave it back to me, it had become four large stones, much more precious than diamonds—incomparably more so, for it is impossible, of course, to make comparisons with what is supernatural, and diamonds seem imperfect counterfeits beside the precious stones which I saw in that vision. On the cross, with exquisite workmanship, were portrayed the five wounds. He told me that henceforward it would always look to me like that, and so it did. I could never see the wood of which it was made, but only these stones." *Saint John of the Cross referred to this type of experience as a "spiritual espousal," stating that Jesus uses this kind of encounter to declare his love for the recipient. But "spiritual espousal" is not the highest level of betrothal between Jesus and the beloved; "spiritual marriage" is the final consummation of love between Christ and a human.* John of the Cross wrote: "In the espousal there is only a mutual agreement and willingness between the two, and the bridegroom graciously gives jewels and ornaments to his espoused. But in marriage there is also a communication and union between the persons." *Teresa of Avila also experienced the spiritual marriage with Jesus. According to Saint John of the Cross, only those who have achieved the highest degree of sanctity are given such a gift, adding that* "it is accordingly the highest state attainable in this life . . ." *Saint Teresa wrote that* "it is all a matter of love united with love." *She went on to write about the actual event and how it took place with her:* "He revealed Himself to me in an imaginary vision [with the eyes of the soul], most interiorly, as on other occasions, and He gave me His right hand: 'Behold this nail. It is a sign that from today onward you will be My bride. Until now, you have not merited this; but henceforward you shall regard My honor not only as that of your Creator and King and God, but as that of My very bride. My honor is yours, and yours, Mine.' This favor produced such an effect upon me that I could not restrain myself but became like a person who is foolish and begged the Lord either to exalt my lowliness or to show me fewer favors, for I really did not think my nature could endure them. For the whole of that day I remained completely absorbed. Since then I have been conscious of receiving great benefits and of still greater confusion and distress when I see that in exchange for such great favors I am doing nothing." (TA)

# Communion with God

"I contain all good in myself, and I distribute to each in season what they need." (GG)

"It is a sign that one desires to be united to Me when they cannot take pleasure in what displeases Me." (GG)

"When I pour forth graces in answer to the prayers of My elect, they do not immediately feel devotion, but I will allow them to experience this sweetness whenever I consider it expedient for them." (GG)

"Fear nothing from now on. Be consoled, take courage, and be at rest. I am the Lord your God. I am your beloved, who has created you by a pure effect of My love. I have chosen you to make you My abode by My grace and to take My delight in you." (GG)

"Whoever knows in his heart that his will is so united to Mine as never to dissent from it—either in prosperity or adversity—and who acts and suffers in all things purely for My glory, may certainly affirm that whatever he learns interiorly is from Me if it is useful to others and not contradictory to scripture." (GG)

*Once, Saint Margaret Mary was shown a religious, and then heard these words:* "Behold this nun who is one only in name. I am on the point of rejecting her from My Heart and abandoning her to herself." *Saint Margaret Mary offered herself to God's divine justice in order to suffer all for this soul, so that the soul would not be abandoned to itself.* (MMA)

"One day after receiving Communion, it seemed most clear to me [Teresa of Avila] that Our Lord sat beside me; and He began to console me with great favors, and He told me among other things: 'See Me here, daughter, for it is I. Give Me your hands.' And it seemed He took them and placed them on His side and said: 'Behold My wounds. You are not without Me. This short life is passing away.'"(TA)

# Confidence

"Acknowledge that you can do nothing without Me, who will never let you lack help, as long as you keep your weakness and your nothingness lost in My strength.'" (MMA)

*When Saint Margaret Mary reflected upon the loss of her confessor, Jesus reproved her, saying:* "What! Am I not sufficient for you, I who am your beginning and end?" (MMA)

"Right after I received Communion . . . Our Lord Jesus Christ appeared to me in an imaginative vision, as He usually does. . . . He told me that now was not the time for rest, but that I should hurry to establish these houses; that He found his rest with the souls living in them; that I should accept as many houses as given me since there were many persons who did not serve Him because they had no place for it. . . . I should insist that the interior peace not be lost through a concern for bodily sustenance; that He would help us so nothing would be lacking . . ." (TA)

"Having been so distressed over [Father Gratian's] health that I couldn't be at peace, and begging the Lord very emphatically one day after Communion that since He had given [Father Gratian] to me He not allow me to be without him, the Lord told me: 'Don't be afraid.'" (TA)

". . .While I was praising Our Lord at night for having granted me so many favors, the Lord said to me: 'What do you ask of Me, my daughter, that I do not do?'" (TA)

"Once when in need, for I didn't know what to do or how to pay some workmen, Saint Joseph, my true father and lord, appeared to me and revealed to me that I would not be lacking, that I should hire them [the workmen]. And so I did, without so much as a penny, and the Lord in ways that amazed those who heard about it provided for me." (TA)

# Devil and Demons

"At another time something else happened to me that frightened me [Teresa of Avila] very much. I was at a place where a certain person died who for many years had lived a wicked life, from what I knew. But he had been sick for two years, and in some things it seems he had made amends. He died without confession, but nevertheless it didn't seem to me he would be condemned. While the body was being wrapped in its shroud, I saw many devils take that body, and it seemed they were playing with it and punishing it. This terrified me, for with large hooks they were dragging it from one devil to the other. Since I saw it buried with the honor and ceremonies accorded to all, I reflected on the goodness of God, how He did not want that soul to be defamed, but wanted the fact that it was His enemy to be concealed. I was half stupefied from what I had seen. During the whole ceremony I didn't see another devil. Afterward when they put the body in the grave, there was such a multitude of them inside ready to take it that I was frantic at the sight of it, and there was need for no small amount of courage to conceal this. I reflected on what they would do to the soul when they had such dominion over the unfortunate body. May it please the Lord that what I have seen—a thing so frightful!—will be seen by all those who are in such an evil state. I think it would prove a powerful help toward their living a good life. All of this gives me greater knowledge of what I owe God and of what He freed me from. I was very frightened until I spoke about it to my confessor, wondering if it was an illusion caused by the devil to defame that soul, although it wasn't considered to be the soul of someone with a very deep Christian spirit. Truly since the vision was not an illusion, it frightens me every time I think of it. . . ." *Then, at a later date, Teresa heard the following:* "Don't neglect to write down what I say, for even though it may not benefit you, it can benefit others." (TA)

"Once, while approaching to receive Communion, I saw with my soul's eyes more clearly than with my bodily eyes two devils whose appearance was abominable. It seems to me their horns were wrapped around the poor priest's throat, and in the host that was going to be given to me I saw my Lord with the majesty I mentioned placed in the priest's hands, which were clearly seen to be His offender's. I understood that that soul was in mortal sin. What would it be, my Lord, to see Your beauty in the midst of such abominable figures? They were as though frightened and terrified in Your presence, for it seems they would have very eagerly fled had You allowed them. This vision caused me such great disturbance I don't know how I was able to receive Communion, and I was left with a great fear, thinking that if the vision had been from God, His Majesty would not have permitted me to see the evil that was in that soul. The Lord Himself told me to pray for him and that He had permitted it so that I might understand the power of the words of consecration and how God does not fail to be present, however evil the priest who recites them, and that I might see His great goodness since He places Himself in those hands of His enemy, and all out of love for me and for everyone. I understood well how much more priests are obliged to be good than are others, how deplorable a thing it is to receive this most Blessed Sacrament unworthily, and how much the devil is lord over the soul in mortal sin." (TA)

*Once, when being afflicted by a demon, Saint Teresa used holy water:* "Then I sprinkled some in the direction of the place where the little demon was standing, and immediately he disappeared and all my troubles went, just as if someone had lifted them from me with his hand. . . . [On another occasion], when I was in an oratory, he [the devil] appeared on my left hand in an abominable form. . . . I was very much afraid and made the sign of the cross as well as I could, whereupon he disappeared, but immediately returned again. This happened twice running and I did not know what to do. But there was some holy water there, so I flung some in the direction of the apparition, and it never came back. . . .From long experience I have learned that there is nothing like holy water to put devils to flight and prevent them from coming back again. They also flee from the cross, but return; so holy water must have great virtue. For my own part, whenever I take it, my soul feels a particular and most notable consolation." (TA)

## Distractions

"When, for love of Me, you do anything with difficulty beyond your strength, I receive it even as if I had absolute need of it. But when you omit anything to take due care of your body, referring all to My glory, I consider it in the same manner as an infirm person would consider some relief that it was impossible for him to do without. Thus I will recompense you for both according to the greatness of My divine munificence." (GG)

"... just after receiving Communion, my mental faculties were so scattered and distracted [that] I couldn't help myself, and I began to envy those who live in deserts and to think that since they don't hear or see anything, they are free of this wandering of the mind. I heard: 'You are greatly mistaken, daughter; rather, the temptations of the devil there are stronger. Be patient, for as long as you live, a wandering mind cannot be avoided.'" (TA)

"Once while thinking of how much more purely one lives when withdrawn from business affairs and how when I am involved in them I make poor progress and commit many faults, I heard: 'It cannot be helped, daughter. Strive to have the right intention and to be detached in all things, and look at Me so that what you do might be done in conformity with what I did.'" (TA)

"After having received Communion and been in this very prayer I'm writing about, I was thinking when I wanted to write something on it of what the soul did during that time. The Lord spoke these words to me: 'It detaches itself from everything, daughter, so as to abide more in Me. It is no longer the soul that lives but I. Since it cannot comprehend what it understands, there is an understanding by not understanding.'" (TA)

# Eucharist

"He who communicates from a pure desire of My glory, as I have said, can never communicate with irreverence." (GG)

"Since you have declared that there is nothing which can separate you from Me, know also that there is nothing in heaven or earth, neither judgment nor justice, which can hinder Me from doing all the good for you which My divine Heart desires." (GG)

"I would rather remain dead in the tomb, so to speak, than deprive a soul who loves Me of the fruit of My liberality. Consider also, that even as the blood which comes from the heart of the pelican gives life to its little ones, so also the soul whom I nourish with the divine food which I present to it, receives a life which will never end." (GG)

"Consider in how small a space [in the Eucharist] I give you My entire divinity and My humanity. Compare the size of this with the size of the human body and judge then the greatness of My love. For as the human body surpasses My body in size—that is to say, the quantity of the species of bread under which My body is contained—so My mercy and charity in this Sacrament reduce Me to this state, that the soul which loves Me is in some sort above Me as the human body is greater than My body." (GG)

*On another occasion Saint Gertrude the Great humbled herself deeply before approaching Holy Communion, in honor and in imitation of the humility of the Son of God in descending into death. Then uniting herself with His descent, she found herself descending to the very depths of Purgatory, and humbling herself still lower, she heard our Lord say to her:* "I will draw you to Me in the Sacrament of the Altar in such a manner that you will draw after you all those who shall perceive the odor of your desire." (GG)

"It is true that those who celebrate [the Holy Sacrifice of the Mass] worthily shall shine in great glory, but the love of him who communicates with pleasure should be judged very differently. There will be one reward for him who approaches with fear and reverence, and another for him who is very diligent in his preparation. But those who habitually celebrate through custom only shall have no share in My gifts." (GG)

*Jesus said:* "All who by their words or persuasions drive away those who are not in mortal sin [from receiving the Eucharist] and thus hinder and interrupt the delight which I find in them, act like a severe master who forbids the children of the king to speak to those their own age who may be poor or beneath them in rank, because he considers it more correct that his pupils should receive the honor due to their dignity than to permit them this enjoyment." "But Lord," *inquired Saint Gertrude,* "if this person formed a firm resolution not to commit this fault any more, would you not pardon her for the past?" *Jesus replied,* "I would not only pardon her, but her actions would be as agreeable to Me as it would be to the king's son if his master allowed him to play with those children from whom he had previously driven him away with such severity." (GG)

# Faults

"I, who am the Son of the Virgin, stand before God the Father for the salvation of the human race. Whenever they commit any fault in their hearts through human frailty, I offer My spotless Heart to the Eternal Father in satisfaction for them. When they sin by their actions, I offer My pierced Hands, and so [also with] regard to the other faults that they commit. Thus My innocence appeases Him and disposes Him to pardon those who do penance for their faults. Therefore it is that I desire My elect should return to Me thanks whenever they have obtained pardon for their faults, because it is through Me that they have obtained it so easily." (GG)

*One night, as Gertrude was occupied in examining her conscience, she remarked that she had a habit of saying* "God knows," *without reflection and without necessity; and having blamed herself very severely for this fault, she asked God to never permit her to use His name lightly again. Our Lord replied lovingly to her:* "Why would you deprive Me of the glory and yourself of the immense reward which you acquire every time you perceive this fault, or any similar one, and seriously endeavor to correct it?" (GG)

"I accept your offering of [your] weak heart and prefer it to a strong one; even as the hunter prefers what he has taken in the chase to tame animals." (GG)

*As Saint Gertrude prayed to God to correct a fault in one of her superiors, she received this reply:* "Do you not know that not only this person, but also all those who have charge of this My beloved community, have some defects, since no one can be entirely free from them in this life? This happens by an excess of My mercy, tenderness and love with which I have chosen this congregation, that by this means their merit may be greatly increased. For it is far more virtuous to submit to a person whose faults are apparent, than to one who always appears perfect." *To this the saint replied:* "Although I am full of joy in perceiving great merit in inferiors, I ardently desire that superiors should be free from faults, and I fear they contract them by their imperfections." *Our Lord answered:* "I, who know all their weaknesses, sometimes permit them, in the diversity of their employments, to be sullied by some stain, because otherwise they might never attain so high a degree of humility. Therefore, as the merit of inferiors is increased both by the perfections and imperfections of their superiors, so the merit of superiors increases by the perfections and imperfections of inferiors, even as the different members of the same body contribute to mutual increase." (GG)

*Saint Margaret Mary was naturally drawn to the love of pleasure and amusement, but no longer enjoyed them, although she sought them eagerly. The painful sight of her Savior after the scourging hindered her from delighting in them, and the following words, with which He reproached her, pierced her to the heart:* "Would you take this pleasure, whereas I never had any and delivered Myself up to every kind of bitterness for love of you and to win your heart?" (MMA)

"Learn that I am a holy master and one that teaches holiness. I am pure and cannot endure the slightest stain. Therefore you must act with simplicity of heart and with an upright and pure intention in My presence. Know that I cannot endure the least want of straightforwardness, and I shall make you understand that if the excess of My love has led Me to constitute Myself your master in order to teach and fashion you after My manner and according to My designs, nevertheless I cannot bear tepid and cowardly souls. And if I am gentle in bearing with your weakness, I shall not be less severe and exact in correcting and punishing your infidelities." (MMA)

*Saint Margaret Mary wrote:* "Although His pure and penetrating (eyes) discover even the smallest faults against charity and humility in order to correct them severely, nevertheless nothing can be compared to a want of obedience either against superiors or the rules, and the smallest reply to superiors, manifesting repugnance to obey, is unbearable to Him in the soul of a religious." (MMA)

*Saint Margaret Mary wrote:* "Yet, however great my faults may be, that sole love of my soul, in accordance with His promise, never deprives me of His divine presence. But He makes it so terrible to me when I have displeased Him, that there is no torment which would not be sweeter to me and to which I would not sacrifice myself a thousand times, rather than bear that divine presence and appear before the sanctity of God with the least stain of sin on my soul." (MMA)

## Fear

*Saint Mechtilde, a friend of Saint Gertrude, once beheld the heart of Saint Gertrude forming a firm and stable bridge, the sides of which appeared to be Jesus' divinity on one side and His humanity on the other. After seeing this, Mechtilde heard these words:* "Those who come to Me by this bridge need to have no apprehension of wandering or of falling; that is to say, all those who receive her counsels and execute them faithfully shall never wander from the right path, which leads to the life of a blessed eternity." (GG)

"I will be your strength . . . fear nothing, but be attentive to My voice and to what I shall require of you that you may be in requisite dispositions for the accomplishment of My designs." (MMA)

*The Lord knew that Saint Margaret Mary always had a horror of being deceived by Satan. He powerfully dispelled her fears when He reassuringly told her:* "What have you to fear in the arms of the Almighty? Could I possibly allow you to perish and deliver you up to your enemies after having constituted Myself your Father, your master and your ruler from your youngest years and given you continual proofs of the loving tenderness of My divine Heart, in which I have even established your dwelling for time and for eternity? As a greater assurance, say what stronger proof of My love you would have, and I will give it to you. But why do you fight against Me, who am your one true and only friend?" (MMA)

*Jesus told Saint Margaret Mary:* "Fear nothing, I shall reign in spite of My enemies and of all who oppose me." (MMA)

## Generosity

*A holy man once asked God what was most pleasing in Saint Gertrude. He was answered that it was* "her generosity of heart." *The man responded,* "As for me, O Lord, I had imagined that what pleased You most in this soul was the perfect humility she had of herself and the high degree of love to which by Your grace she had attained." *Our Lord replied:* "This generosity of heart is of such value and so great a good that the height of perfection may be obtained through it. By means of it [a chosen soul] is prepared at all times for receiving gifts of great value, which prevents her from attaching her heart to anything which could either impede Me or displease Me." (GG)

*When someone asked Saint Gertrude to tell about the secret graces God had recently given to her, Gertrude asked the Blessed Virgin Mary what she should do.* Mary said, "Give freely what you possess, for My Son is rich enough to repay all that you expend for His glory." *Saint Gertrude asked Jesus as well, and He replied,* "Give My money to the bank, that when I come I may receive it with usury [interest]." (Cf. Luke 19:23) *And thus she learned that the reasons which she had considered good, and even inspired by the Spirit of God, were merely human, so that from henceforth she imparted more freely what was revealed to her.* (GG)

"I remained in the kind of prayer I now have, that of keeping my soul present with the Blessed Trinity. And it seemed to me that the Person of the Father drew me to Himself and spoke very pleasant words. Among them . . . He told me: 'I gave you My Son, and the Holy Spirit, and this Blessed Virgin. What can you give Me?'" (TA)

*Saint Margaret Mary wrote:* ". . . in order to honor His fast in the desert, He [Our Lord] willed that I should fast fifty days on bread and water. But not being allowed to do this in case I should appear singular, He gave me to understand that it would be equally agreeable to Him if I were to remain days without drinking, in order thereby to honor the burning thirst that His Sacred Heart had always endured for the salvation of sinners, as also that which He suffered on the tree of the cross." (MMA)

# Grace

*Jesus gave three reasons to Saint Margaret Mary why He wanted her to write of her spiritual experiences:* "In the first place I desire this of you, in order to show you that I battle and render useless all the precautions which I have allowed you to take, to hide the profusion of graces with which I have taken pleasure in enriching so poor and miserable a creature as yourself. You should never lose sight thereof, so that you may render Me continual thanks for them. Secondly, it is to teach you that you must in no way appropriate them to yourself, nor be reserved in distributing them to others, since I desire to make use of your heart as of a channel through which to pour these graces into souls according to My designs, by means drawing many from the abyss of perdition, as I will show you hereafter. Thirdly, it is to manifest that I am the eternal Truth and that the graces which I have bestowed in you are open to every kind of examination and test." (MMA)

*Whenever Saint Margaret became conscious of a fault, Jesus would come to her assistance and like a good father would stretch out His loving arms towards her and say:* "Now you know full well that you cannot do anything without Me." (MMA)

"[Jesus] willed that I should await all from Him; and if I happened to seek some little consolation, fresh torments and desolation were the only alleviation He permitted me to find. I have always looked upon this as one of the greatest graces my God has granted me." (MMA)

"My sovereign Lord also made known to me that when He was about to abandon any of those souls for whom He wished me to suffer, He would place me in the state of a reprobate

soul, making me feel the desolation in which it finds itself at
the hour of death. I have never experienced anything more
terrible and can find no words to describe it." (MMA)

"O beloved Soul, do you know who it is that employs
My love? He whose heart is pure and empty of every other
love." (CoG)

*Saint Catherine of Genoa wrote,* "At first the assistance [of
God] is very evident, that he [man] may with love persevere
and form the habit of doing spiritual works. Then, by degrees,
God withdraws these supports whenever He finds man strong
enough to endure the battle. The greater strength he has at the
beginning, the greater suffering he may look for toward the
end, although God always assists him according to his necessi-
ties. Yet He does this far more secretly than openly and never
ceases but at death." (CoG)

"You cannot live without love, for it is your life, both in
this world and in the other. Even those who are in Heaven,
their home, know it [love] only according to the measure of
grace and charity they have had in this life." (CoG)

*As Gertrude prayed for a person who complained of hav-*
*ing less devotion on the days on which she received Communion*
*than on others, Our Lord said to her:* "This has not happened
by chance but by a particular providence which inspires feelings of devotion at unexpected times, to elevate the heart of
man, which is so enslaved by the body. But on festivals and at
the time of Communion I withdraw this grace, preferring to
occupy the hearts of My elect with good desires or humility,
and this may be more advantageous to their welfare than the
grace of devotion." (GG)

"Faith remains without merit and unfruitful when human reason has perceived what it believes." (GG)

*Jesus said to Saint Gertrude:* "I will use you to draw many to Me." *She replied:* "How can you lead others to You through me, since I am such an unworthy creature and have almost lost the talent I once had of instructing and conversing with others?" *Our Lord answered:* "If you now had that facility of speaking, perhaps you would think that it was by this you won souls. Therefore I have deprived [you] of it in part, that you may acknowledge that the grace which you possess of touching the hearts of others comes from My special grace, and not from the power and attractiveness of your words." (GG)

"Behold, I promise to preserve inviolate the gifts which I have bestowed on you. However, if I suspend their effects for a time by way of dispensation, I oblige myself, by the omnipotence, wisdom and love of the Trinity, in which I live and reign true God through all ages, to recompense you afterwards threefold." (GG)

*Saint Margaret Mary wrote that God showed her* "the horrible sight of a soul in mortal sin, and the grievousness of it, attacking, as it does, a goodness infinitely loving and being such a great insult to Him." (MMA)

"I was reflecting upon how arduous a life this is that deprives us of being always in that wonderful company [of God], and I said to myself, 'Lord, give me some means by which I can put up with this life.' He replied: 'Think, daughter, of how after it is finished you will not be able to serve Me in ways you can now. Eat for Me and sleep for Me, and let everything you do be for Me, as though you no longer lived but I; for this is what Saint Paul was speaking of.'" (TA)

"When, at night, I took off those accursed liveries of Satan, namely all that worldly attire, the instruments of his malice, my sovereign master presented himself to me torn and disfigured as of the time of His scourging, and with bitter reproaches, He said that it was my vanity which had reduced Him to that state, and that I was wasting most precious time of which He would demand a rigorous account from me at the hour of my death. He added that I betrayed and persecuted Him, regardless of the many proofs He had given me of His love and of His desire that I should render myself conformable to Him. This made such a deep impression upon me and caused such painful wounds in my heart that I wept bitterly, and it would be difficult for me to express all that I suffered or what passed within me." (MMA)

*On one occasion Saint Margaret Mary yielded to vanity in speaking of herself, and God called her to account, saying with a look of severity:* "What have you to boast of, O dust and ashes, since of yourself you are but nothingness and misery, of which you should never lose sight, and so should ever remain buried in this abyss of your nothingness! In order that the greatness of My gifts may not lead you to forget what you are, I will set before you your portrait" *He then showed her a repulsive picture of herself that revealed to her the true nature of her being.* (MMA)

"For whoever has perfect will to praise Me, if he could, more than all the world, or to love Me, thank Me, suffer with Me, or exercise himself in the most perfect manner in all kinds of virtue, will certainly be recompensed by divine liberality more advantageously than one who has actually performed many other things." (GG)

*As Saint Gertrude was deprived for some time of the accustomed visits of Jesus, she ventured to inquire why the favor was withheld, though she neither felt discouragement nor depression in consequence. Jesus replied:* "When a person looks at anyone who is close to them, the proximity often prevents them from seeing distinctly. For example, when a friend meets his friend and embraces him, this close union deprives him of the pleasure of looking at him." *Saint Gertrude understood by these words that we often merit more when deprived of sensible grace, provided that we do not become less fervent in the practice of good works.* (GG)

# Heaven

"As time went on, it happened—and continues to happen sometimes—that the Lord showed me greater secrets. There is no way in which the soul can see more than what is manifested, nor is this possible, so my soul never saw more than what the Lord wanted to show it each time. What He revealed was so great that the least part of it would have been sufficient to leave me marveling and very proficient in considering and judging all the things of life as little. I should like to be able to explain something about the least of what I came to know, and in thinking about how this can be done, I find that it is impossible. In just the difference between the light we see and the one represented there, although all is light, there is no comparison. Next to that light, the sun's brilliance seems to be something very blurred. In sum, the imagination, however keen it may be, cannot paint or sketch what this light is like, or any of the things the Lord gave me knowledge of.

He bestows along with this knowledge a delight so sublime
as to be indescribable, for all the senses rejoice to such a high
degree and in such sweetness that the delight cannot be exag-
gerated—so it's better not to say any more. Once, for more
than an hour, since it doesn't seem to me that He left my side,
the Lord was showing me admirable things in this way. He
said to me: 'See, daughter, what those who are against Me
lose. Don't neglect to tell them.'" (TA)

"On occasion there come over me such ardent desires to
receive Communion that I don't think they could be exag-
gerated. . . . When I reached the church, a great rapture came
upon me. It seemed to me I saw the heavens open, not just an
entrance as I have seen before. A throne was shown to me . . .
and above it another throne where the divinity was. Although
I didn't see the divinity, I knew with an indescribable knowledge that It was there. Seemingly some animals were holding
up the throne . . . I wondered if they were the Evangelists. But
what the throne was like or who was on it, I didn't see—only
a great multitude of angels. They seemed to me to be incomparably more beautiful than those I had seen in Heaven. I
wondered if they were seraphim or cherubim because they
were very different in glory. It seemed they were afire; the difference is great. And the glory I then experienced in myself
cannot be put in writing or described, nor could anyone who
hadn't experienced it imagine what it is like. I understood
that everything desirable is brought together there, yet I didn't
see anything. I was told, I don't know by whom, that what
I could do there was understand that I couldn't understand
anything and reflect upon how in comparison with that glory
everything else was nothing at all. As a consequence, my soul
was afterward ashamed to see that it could be detained by
any created thing. How much more [shameful] if it were to

become attached to it, for all things seemed to me like an ant-hill." (TA)

# Holiness

"For as the services which we render in adversity are far more esteemed than those which are rendered in prosperity, so I esteem far more the services which are offered to Me now, when the world offends Me so much more than at any other time." (GG)

"Ah!" *exclaimed Gertrude,* "Teach me, O best of teachers, how to perform even one action perfectly in memory of Your passion." *Our Lord replied:* "When you are praying, extend your arms to represent the manner in which I extended Mine to God My Father in My passion and do this for the salvation of every member of the Church, in union with the love with which I stretched out My arms on the cross. If anyone prays thus with his hands extended, without fear of contradiction, he pays Me the same honor as one would do solemnly enthroned as a king." (GG)

"Although My sensitive nature felt keenly all humiliations and mortifications, I [Saint Margaret Mary] nevertheless had an insatiable desire for them, and I was constantly urged by My divine master to ask for them." (MMA)

"While one is alive, progress doesn't come from trying to enjoy Me more but by trying to do My will." (TA)

# Hope

"As a tender mother soothes the troubles of her little one by her kisses and embraces, so do I desire to soothe all your pain and grief by the sweet murmur of My loving words." (GG)

"Your pure intention of doing everything for Me alone will be a wick, a light of which will be most pleasing to Me." (GG)

"Once in comforting me, He told me with much love that I shouldn't be anxious, that in this life we cannot always be in a stable condition, that sometimes the soul will experience fervor and at other times be without it, that sometimes it will have disturbances and at other times have quiet, and again temptations; but that it should hope in Him and not be afraid." (TA)

"Once while desiring to render some service to our Lord, I was thinking about how little I was able to do for Him, and I said to myself: 'Why, Lord, do You desire my works?' He answered: 'In order to see your will, daughter.'" (TA)

"In the resurrection, when the body will be raised incorruptible, each of its members will receive a special recompense for the labors and actions which it has performed in My name and for My love. But the soul will receive an incomparably greater reward for all the holy affections it has entertained for My love, for its compunction, and even for having animated the body for My service." (GG)

"Why be surprised that a father should allow his son to ask him repeatedly for a crown, if he laid by a hundred marks of gold for him each time the request was made? Neither should you be surprised if I defer answering your petition, because each time that you implore My aid by the least word, or even in thought, I prepare a recompense for you in eternity of infinitely greater value than a hundred marks of gold." (GG)

"Listen then, O Soul, My beloved! Listen to My voice. Open your ears to your Lord who so much loves you, who is ever caring for you and who alone is your salvation!" (CoG)

"Know then in the first place, that I am God, with whom there is no change. Know too that I loved man before I created him. I loved him with a love that is infinite, pure, simple and sincere, and without any cause. It is impossible that I should not love those whom I have created and designed for My glory, each in his own degree." (CoG)

"If one who had not lost faith should desire to see the effects of this work which is accomplished in man by that spark of love which infuses into his heart, be assured that he would be so inflamed by love that he could not live, for so great would be its power that he would melt away and be no more. Though men are for the most part forever in ignorance of it, yet for this hidden love, you see those who abandon the world, leave their possessions, friends and kindred, and hold in abhorrence all other loves and joys. . . . You see this love transform beasts into men, men into angels, and angels becoming God, as it were, by participation. You see men changed from earthly into heavenly [beings], and devoting themselves with both soul and body to the practice of spiritual things. Their whole life and manner of speech are altered, and they do and say the contrary of what was formerly their custom. All are surprised at this, and yet it seems good to all, and men are almost envious of it." (CoG)

*Saint Catherine of Genoa wrote of God's love:* "This love makes every affliction and contradiction appear sweet." (CoG)

"But that love which you desire to know is beyond your comprehension, for it has neither form nor limit. Neither can you know it through the intellect, for it is not intelligible. It is in part made known by its effects, which are small or great in proportion to the measure of love which is brought into action." (CoG)

"Love is God Himself, who cannot be comprehended except by the wonderful effects of the great love which He is ever manifesting, and which can neither be estimated nor imagined. And when I reveal to the Soul but one spark of My pure love, she is constrained to return Me that love, whose power compels her to do her all for Me, even if need be, to suffer torture and a thousand deaths. How much love may be infused into the hearts of men can be learned from what men have done for love of Me." (CoG)

"My love so delights the Soul that it destroys every other joy which can be possessed by man here below." (CoG)

*While preparing to make her annual confession and being anxious to discover her sins, Jesus told Saint Margaret Mary:* "Why do you torment yourself? Do what lies in your power; I will supply what is wanting. In this sacrament I ask for nothing so much as for a contrite and humble heart which, with a sincere will never to offend Me again, accuses itself frankly.

I then pardon without delay, and so follows perfect amendment." (MMA)

"Once while I was experiencing great distress over having offended God, He said to me: 'All your sins are before Me as though they were not. In the future make every effort, for your trials are not over.'" (TA)

"Once when I was looking at a picture of the great Saint Francis de Sales [the founder of the religious order to which God was calling her], it seemed to me that he called me his daughter, and cast upon me a look so full of paternal love that I no longer regarded him otherwise than as 'my good father.'" (MMA)

"Does not the Catholic faith teach you that I bestow myself, with all the riches that are contained in the treasures of My divinity and My humanity, for the salvation of those who communicate [receive Holy Communion] even once? The more people receive Communion, the more their beatitude is increased and perfected." (GG)

"O bountiful Lord!" *inquired Gertrude,* "How can you give graces so full of consolation to one so unworthy to receive them?" *Jesus replied:* "My love compels Me." *Then she asked,* "Where are the stains which I contracted lately by my impatience, and which I manifested by my words?" *Jesus replied,* "The fire of My love has consumed them entirely, for I efface all the stains which I meet within the souls whom I visit by My free and loving grace." (GG)

"My divine Heart, understanding human inconstancy and frailty, desires with incredible ardor continually to be invited, either by your words, or at least by some other sign, to operate and accomplish in you what you are not able to accomplish yourself." (GG)

"Whenever anyone from gratitude and devotion gives Me thanks for having become man for his sake, I also incline to him by a pure movement of My goodness. I offer from My inmost Heart all the fruit and merit of My humanity to God the Father, that the eternal beatitude of this person may be doubled." (GG)

# Humility

*Saint Gertrude once had a vision in which she saw the Lord descending from his throne to comfort sinners. She saw streams of his grace flow through Heaven and the saints thanking Him for his mercy with songs of praise and joy. The Lord told Saint Gertrude:* "Consider how agreeable this concert of praise is, not only to My ears, but even to My most loving Heart. Beware for the future how you desire so importunately to be separated from the body merely for the sake of being delivered from the flesh in which I pour forth so freely the gifts of My grace, for the more unworthy they are to whom I condescend, the more I merit to be glorified for it by all creatures." (GG)

"Each time that you acknowledge your unworthiness of My gifts, and confide fully in My mercy, you acquit yourself of the debts you owe Me for these benefits." (GG)

*As she prayed for another person who desired divine conso-lation, Saint Gertrude received this reply:* "She is herself the obstacle which prevents her from receiving the sweetness of

My grace; for when I draw My elect to Me by the interior attractions of My love, they who remain obstinate in the exercise of their own judgment place the same impediment to it as one would who closed his nostrils with his robe to prevent himself from smelling a delicious perfume. But he who, for love of Me, renounces his own judgment to follow that of another, acquires a merit all the greater for acting contrary to his inclination, because he is not merely humble, but perfectly victorious; for the apostle says none will be crowned 'except he strives lawfully.'"(Cf. 2 Tim. 2:5) (GG)

*After recommitting herself to entering religious life, Saint Margaret Mary noted:* "He now changed His manner toward me, making me see the beauty of virtue, especially of the three vows of poverty, chastity, and obedience, and telling me that by observing them one becomes holy. This He said because when in prayer, I often begged Him to make me a saint." (MMA)

"While I was at the monastery in Toledo, some were advising me that I shouldn't give a burying-place to anyone who had not belonged to the nobility. The Lord said to me: 'You will grow very foolish, daughter, if you look at the world's laws. Fix your eyes on Me, poor and despised by the world. Will the great ones of the world, perhaps, be great before Me? Or, are you to be esteemed for lineage or for virtue?'" (TA)

"With regard to the fear about whether or not I was in the state of grace, He told me: 'Daughter, light is very different from darkness. I am faithful. Nobody will be lost unknowingly. They who find security in spiritual favors will be deceived. True security is the testimony of a good conscience. But people should not think that through their own efforts they can be in light or that they can do anything to prevent the night, because these states depend upon My grace. The best help for holding on to the light is to understand that you can do nothing and that it comes from Me. For even though you may be in light, at the moment I withdraw, the night will come. This is true humility: to know what *you* can do and what *I* can do.'" (TA)

"Once . . . God seemed so present to me that I thought of Saint Peter's words: 'You are Christ, Son of the Living God.' For God was thus living in my soul. This presence is not like other visions, because it is accompanied by such living faith that one cannot doubt that the Trinity is in our souls by presence, power and essence. It is an extremely beneficial thing to understand this truth. Since I was amazed to see such majesty in something so lowly as my soul, I heard: 'It is not lowly, daughter, for it is made in My image.'" (TA)

## Jesus

*On Good Friday, as they made a commemoration of Our Lord's burial after the Office, Gertrude implored Jesus to bury Himself in her soul and to abide there forever. Our Lord replied,* "I will serve as a stone to close the gates of your senses. I will place My affections there as soldiers to guard this stone, to defend your heart against all hurtful affections, and to work in you My divine power for My eternal glory." (GG)

*On the return of the community from a procession, Gertrude heard Jesus speak these words to the Father from a crucifix which had been carried at the front of the procession:* "Eternal Father, I come with My whole army to supplicate you, under the same form in which I reconciled you to the human race." *And these words were received by the Eternal Father with as much complacence as if a satisfaction had been offered to Him which surpassed a thousand times all the sins of men. Then she saw God the Father taking up the image of the crucifix into the clouds with these words:* "This is a sign of the covenant which I have made with the earth." ( Cf. Gen. 9) (GG)

"I take pleasure in the veneration offered to My cross when it is offered purely for My love. Thus it may serve to renew the memory of the love and fidelity with which I endured the bitterness of My passion, and when there is an ardent desire to imitate the example of My passion." (GG)

"All those who meditate frequently on the vision of My divine face attracted by the desires of love . . . shall reflect the light of My countenance in a special manner in eternity." (GG)

"When I give great favors in return for a little devotion, those on whom I bestow them are obliged to profit by them. If they fail to do so, they will lose the fruit from them, but the ornament of My gratuitous goodness in bestowing them will always appear on them for My praise and glory." (GG)

## Love of God

"May the full tide of your affections flow to Me, so that all your pleasure, your hope, your joy, your grief, your fear and every other feeling may be sustained by My love!" (GG)

"When I behold anyone in his agony who has thought of Me with pleasure, or who has performed any works deserving of reward, I appear to him at the moment of death with a countenance so full of love and mercy, that he repents from his inmost heart for having ever offended Me, and he is saved by this repentance. I desire, therefore, that My elect should acknowledge this mercy by thanksgivings, and that they should praise Me for this amongst the great number of benefits which they receive from Me." (GG)

*Once, as Gertrude meditated on her own sinfulness, she began to question how she could be agreeable in the sight of God, who must see only a thousand imperfections. But Our Lord consoled her by this reply:* "Love makes all agreeable." (GG)

"See, My daughter, whether you can find a father whose love for his only son has prompted him to take such great care of him or show him such delicate proofs of his love as are those which I have given and will yet give to you of Mine. For from your tenderest years it has borne kindly with you and has trained and formed you after My own manner, awaiting you patiently, without being disheartened in the midst of all your resistance. Remember, therefore, if ever you should be unmindful of the gratitude you owe Me and not refer the glory of all to Me, it would be the means of making this inexhaustible source of all good dry up for you." (MMA)

*Once when Saint Margaret Mary ardently longed for Jesus in Holy Communion, He appeared to her when she was carrying away some sweepings and said:* "My daughter, I have heard your sighs, and the desires of your heart are so pleasing to Me that if I had not [already] instituted My divine sacrament of love, I would do so now for your sake in order to have the pleasure of dwelling in your soul and of taking My repose of love in your heart." (MMA)

"Why are you disturbed, little sinner? Am I not your God? Don't you see how badly I was treated there? If you love Me, why don't you grieve for Me?" (TA)

"I would draw him [man] to Me by love and faith alone, to which fear and self-interest are opposed, because they spring from the love of self, which cannot coexist with that pure and simple love which alone must absorb man. . . ." (CoG)

"The true love which you are striving, O Soul, to comprehend . . . is seen only when I have consumed the imperfections of man by every mode of human misery, both exterior and interior." (CoG)

*Regarding the three kinds of work done with love, Saint Catherine of Genoa wrote:* "In this first state of love [when one performs good works either for the benefit of himself or his neighbor], God causes man to undertake many and various useful and necessary works, which he performs with a pious intention. The works of the second state of love are done in God. These are done with no view either to the advantage of one's self or of one's neighbor, but rest in God with no motive in him who does them. Here man perseveres through the habits of virtue which he has formed, although God has deprived him of that share in them which gave him aid and pleasure. This work is more perfect than the other, in that there were many motives which nourished both soul and body. The works done by love are more perfect than the other two, because man has no part whatever in them. Love has so subdued and conquered him that he finds himself drowned in the sea of love and knows not where he is, but is lost in himself and left without the power to act. In this case it is love itself which works in man, and its works are works of perfection inasmuch as they are not wrought by human power and are works of sanctifying grace, and God accepts them all." (CoG)

"Creatures like these [those who are consumed by God's love] no longer take part in the things of this world, save through necessity, and then as if they knew them not. They are always occupied interiorly, and this prevents their being nourished by temporal things. God sends into their hearts rays and flames of love so subtle and penetrating that they know not where they are, but remain silently plunged in the serene depths of that love. And if God did not sometimes deprive them of this vehement love, the soul could not remain in the body." (CoG)

# Mary

*Saint Gertrude once saw the Blessed Virgin with a parchment in her hand on which the words "She will intercede" were written in letters of gold, and this she presented to her Son by the ministry of angels.* He replied lovingly: "I give you full power, by My omnipotence, to be propitious to all who invoke your aid in whatever manner is most pleasing to you." (GG)

"My Heart was drawn more toward him [Saint John the Apostle] for each act of devotion he offered to My Mother." (GG)

*Gertrude offered herself to God during her prayer and asked how He desired her to occupy herself at that time.* He replied: "Honor My Mother who is seated at My side, and employ yourself in praising her." (GG)

*Mary once said to Saint Gertrude:* "Call my beloved Jesus my first-born rather than my only begotten, for I brought Him forth first, but after Him, or rather by Him, I have you His brethren and my children when I adopted you as such by the maternal affection which I have for you." (GG)

*On the glorious feast of the Nativity of the Blessed Virgin, Saint Gertrude, having said as many Ave Marias as she had remained days in her mother's womb, offered them to her [the Virgin Mary] devoutly, and inquired what merit they would have who performed a like devotion. The Virgin replied:* "They will merit a special share in the joys which I possess in Heaven, which are continually renewed, and in the virtues with which the ever-blessed and glorious Trinity adorns me." (GG)

*The most Blessed Virgin appeared to Saint Margaret Mary and said:* "Take courage, my daughter, in the health which I restore to you at the will of my divine Son, for you have yet a long and painful way to go, always upon the cross, pierced with nails and thorns and torn with scourges. But fear nothing. I will not abandon you and I promise you my protection." (MMA)

*Saint Margaret Mary was at a loss regarding how to prevent her family from making her enter the order of the Ursulines. She prayed and had several Masses said in honor of the Blessed Mother, who lovingly consoled her, saying:* "Fear nothing, you shall be my true daughter, and I will always be your good mother." (MMA)

*When she was very young and reciting the rosary while sitting in a chair, the Blessed Mother appeared to Saint Margaret Mary and gave her the following gentle reprimand:* "I am surprised, My daughter, that you serve me so negligently!" (MMA)

*Saint Teresa of Avila wrote:* "He told me that immediately after His resurrection, He went to see our Lady because she then had great need and that the pain she experienced so absorbed and transpierced her soul that she did not return immediately to herself to rejoice in that joy. By this I understood how different was this other transpiercing, the one of my soul. But what must have been that transpiercing of the Blessed Virgin's soul! He also said that He had remained a long time with her because it was necessary in order to console her." (TA)

## Mercy

*Once when Saint Gertrude was surprised to find her soul still pure despite her faults, the Lord told her:* "Do you think that I possess less power than I have bestowed on My creatures? I have given to the material sun such virtue that a discolored garment exposed to its rays will recover its former whiteness and become even brighter than before. How much more can I, who am the creator of the sun, by directing My looks upon a sinner, remove all his stains, purifying him by the fire of My love from every spot?" (GG)

"If I conduct My spouse to a banquet and I perceive before she enters that her attire is disheveled, will I not draw her aside to a retired place and arrange it with My own hands, that I may introduce her with honor?" (GG)

"Is the sinner deprived of Your grace like someone who goes from light into darkness?" *Saint Gertrude once asked. The*

*Lord replied:* "No, for although the sinner hides My divine light from him, still My goodness will not fail to leave him some ray to guide him to eternal life. This light will increase whenever he hears Mass with devotion or approaches the sacraments." (GG)

*Saint Gertrude, having one day heard a sermon on the justice of God, was so overcome by fear that she dared not approach Communion. But God in His mercy reassured her by these words:* "If you will not look with the eyes of your soul on the many mercies which I have bestowed on you, open at least the eyes of your body and behold Me before you enclosed in a little pyx, and know assuredly that the rigor of My justice is even thus limited within the bounds of the mercy which I exercise toward men in the dispensation of this sacrament." (GG)

*After Communion, Saint Gertrude asked our Lord to release as many souls from Purgatory as she could divide the Host into particles in her mouth. He said to her:* "In order that you may know that My mercy is above all My works and that the abyss of My mercy cannot be exhausted, I am ready to grant you, through the merit of this life-giving Sacrament, more than you dare ask Me." (GG)

"Do you not know that I look on you with eyes of mercy whenever you suffer any pain of body or mind?" (GG)

*Saint Gertrude prayed for a person who had persecuted her, and received this reply:* "As it would be impossible for anyone to have his foot pierced through without his heart sympathizing in its suffering, so My paternal goodness cannot fail to look with eyes of mercy on those who, while they groan under their infirmities and feel their need of pardon, are nevertheless moved by a holy charity to pray for the welfare of their neighbor." (GG)

*When contemplating the Holy Face one day, Saint Gertrude asked the Lord's mercy for all her sins which had caused His face to be disfigured. The Lord appeared to her, raised His hand in blessing and said:* "I grant you, by My mercy, the pardon and remission of all your sins and that you may truly amend your life. In return, I ask that each day during this year you will perform this action in union with, and in memory of, the mercy by which I grant you this indulgence. . . . Oh, what abundant benedictions I will pour forth on him who returns to Me at the end of this year with works of charity exceeding the number of his sins!" (GG)

*When Saint Margaret Mary was overwhelmed with amazement on seeing that Jesus was not repulsed by so many falls and infidelities which she saw in herself, He gave her this answer:* "It is because I desire to make of you, as it were, a compound of My love and of My mercy." (MMA)

*Jesus once showed Saint Margaret Mary the chastisement He was about to inflict on some souls, but she cast herself at His feet and said:* "O My Savior, I beseech You rather to wreak your vengeance upon me and blot me out of the Book of Life than to permit these souls which have cost you so dear to perish!"

*He answered:* "But they love you not and cease not to afflict you."

*Saint Margaret Mary replied:* "It matters not, My God, provided they love you. I will not cease entreating you to pardon them."

*Jesus said:* "Let Me do as I will, I can bear with them no longer."

*Embracing Him still more closely, Saint Margaret Mary replied:* "No, My Lord, I will not leave You until You have pardoned them."

*Jesus said:* "I will do so if you will be surety for them."

*Margaret replied:* "Yes, My God, but I will pay You only with Your own goods, which are the treasures of Your Sacred Heart." *With that Jesus indicated He was satisfied.* (MMA)

*Saint Margaret Mary wrote in her autobiography:* ". . . like a wise and experienced director, He [Jesus] occasionally took pleasure in contradicting My wishes, making me enjoy when I would have wished to suffer. But I acknowledge that both one and the other came from Him, and that all the favors He bestowed upon me proceeded purely from His mercy, for no creature ever resisted Him so much as I have done, not only by my infidelities, but also by the fear I had of being deceived. Hundreds of times I was astonished that He did not punish so much resistance by casting me into an abyss and annihilating me." (MMA)

"He told me that now was not the time for rest, but that I should hurry to establish these [new monasteries] . . . that the sick especially should be cared for; that a prioress who did not provide for and favor the sick was like Job's friends. . . ." (TA)

"When a brother-in-law of mine died suddenly and I was deeply grieved because he hadn't had the chance to go to confession, it was told to me in prayer that my sister would die this way, that I should go to her and try to get her to prepare herself for such an event. I told my confessor, and since he didn't allow me to go, I heard the message at other times. When he learned of this, he told me to go there and that there was nothing to lose. She lived in a small village. I went and without telling her about the locution, enlightened her as I could about everything and got her to confess very frequently and in all events to take care of her soul. She was very good and she did so. Within four or five days after she had gained this habit and become very conscientious, she died without seeing anyone or being able to confess. Happily, since she had acquired the habit, little more than eight days had passed since she had gone to confession. News of her death brought me great joy. She remained a very short while in Purgatory. I don't think more than eight days passed when the Lord appeared to me after I received Communion and wanted me to see how he brought her to glory. In all those years from the time He told me until she died, I didn't forget what had been made known to me, nor did my companion. As soon as my sister died, my companion came to me very much amazed to see how the revelation had been fulfilled. May God be praised forever who takes such care of souls so that they be not lost." (TA)

## Obedience

*Saint Margaret Mary complained to Jesus of the great repugnance she felt about writing. Jesus said:* "Continue My daughter, continue: neither more nor less will come of this repugnance. My will must be accomplished." (MMA)

"Do you not know that I am the eternal memory of My heavenly Father, by whom nothing is forgotten and before whom the past and the future are as the present? Write therefore, without fear, according as I shall dictate to you, and I promise you the unction of My grace in order that I may be glorified." (MMA)

*After engaging in penances beyond that which she had been authorized to do, Saint Margaret Mary heard the voice of Saint Frances DeSales:* "What is this, my daughter? Do you think to please God in surpassing the limits of obedience, which is the foundation and principal support of this Congregation, and not austerities?" (MMA)

*After Saint Margaret Mary told her superior that she should not fear accepting her into the religious community, the superior ordered Margaret Mary to ask, as a proof of security, that God would render her useful to holy religion by the exact observance of all that is prescribed. Jesus replied:* "I shall render you more useful than she thinks, but in a manner known at present only to Me. Henceforth, I shall adjust My graces to the spirit of your rule, to the will of your superiors and to your weakness, so that you must regard as suspicious everything that might withdraw you from the exact observance of your rule, which it is My will that you should prefer before all else. Further, I am satisfied that you should prefer the will of your superiors to Mine whenever they may forbid you to do what I command you. Suffer them to act as they please with you; I shall know well how to find means for the accomplishment of My designs, even though they may appear to be opposed and contrary to it. I reserve for Myself only the guidance of your interior, and especially of your heart, for, having established within it the empire of My pure love, I will never yield it to others." (MMA)

"Be assured that I am not by any means offended by all these struggles and the opposition you make Me through obedience [to your superiors] for which I gave My life, but I will teach you that I am absolute master of My gifts as also My creatures, and nothing will be able to prevent Me from carrying out My designs. Therefore, not only do I desire that you should do what your superiors command, but also that you should do nothing at all that I order you without their consent. I love obedience, and without it no one can please me." (MMA)

"You deceive yourself in thinking [you can] please Me by actions and mortifications chosen by self-will which, rather than yield, prefer to make superiors bend their will to it. Oh! Be assured that I reject all such things as fruits corrupted by self-will, which I abhor in the soul of a religious. I would rather that she should take all her little comforts through obedience than overburden herself with austerities and fast through her self-will." (MMA)

"Another time when I was taking [the discipline] for the holy souls in Purgatory and wanted to exceed the permission given me, they immediately surrounded me, complaining that I was striking them. This made me resolve to die rather than overstep, ever so little, the limits imposed by obedience. [Jesus] afterwards made me do penance for my fault." (MMA)

*After taking the discipline as she had been ordered, Saint Margaret Mary heard Jesus say:* "This is My share," *but as she still continued beyond what obedience allowed, He added:* "And that is the devil's." *Saint Margaret Mary recognized her mistake and ceased at once.* (MMA)

*After Jesus showed Saint Margaret Mary His divine Heart, together with the particular faults which had irritated Him and all that she should have to suffer in order to appease His just anger, she shuddered from head to foot and did not have the courage to make the sacrifices that were being asked of her. Jesus appeared to her and said:* "It is hard for you to kick against the goad of My justice! But since you have made so much resistance in order to avoid the humiliations that you would have to suffer in this sacrifice, I will give them to you twofold. I asked [of] you merely a secret sacrifice, but now it shall be public at a time and in a manner beyond all human calculation, and accomplished by such humiliating circumstances, that they will be a source of confusion to you for the rest of your life, as well in your own sight as in that of others, that you may understand what it is to resist God." (MMA)

*Her superior directed Saint Margaret Mary to ask God to restore Margaret Mary to perfect health for the space of five months so that the superior would be assured that what took place in the saint was the work of the Spirit of God. The saint presented the superior's written note to Jesus, who replied:* "I promise you, My daughter, that as a proof of the good spirit by which you are led, I would have given her as many years of health as she has asked, and any other assurances she might have required." (MMA)

*Saint Margaret Mary immediately and joyfully complied with her superior's order to attend a retreat despite the fact that she was shivering with a fever. No sooner had she shut herself up alone with Jesus—laying prostrate on the ground and shivering with cold and pain—than He appeared to her, raised her up with caresses, and said:* "At last you are wholly mine and given up entirely to My care. Therefore I intend to give you back in perfect health to those who have thus placed you sick in My hands." (MMA)

*Teresa of Avila wrote:* "Once while thinking about the severe penance [another woman] performed and about how, because of the desires for penance the Lord sometimes gives me, I could have done more were it not for obedience to my confessors, I thought it might be better not to obey them any longer in this matter. The Lord told me: 'That's not so; you are walking on a good and safe path. Do you see all the penance she does? I value your obedience more.'" (TA)

# Prayer

*Saint Gertrude inquired of God what advantage some of her friends had gained by her prayers since they did not seem better for them. Jesus replied:* "Do not be surprised if you do not see the fruits of your prayers with your bodily eyes, because I dispose of them according to My eternal wisdom, to greater advantage. And know that the more you pray for anyone, the happier they will become, because no prayer of faith can remain unfruitful, although [you] do not know in what manner the fruit will come." (GG)

"If in My inscrutable wisdom I do not hear your prayers exactly as you desire, I do so in a manner more useful for you, though human frailty prevents you from seeing this." (GG)

*Saint Gertrude, inquiring about aridity in prayer, asked,* "Lord, what benefit will they gain from these graces who do not perceive them by any interior sweetness?" *He replied:* "When a nobleman bestows an orchard on a friend, he does not at once taste the fruit, as he must wait until it ripens. Thus, when I pour forth precious gifts on a soul, she does not perceive their sweetness until she exercises exterior virtues.

But when the skin of earthly pleasures and consolations is removed, then she can taste the interior consolation." (GG)

*As Saint Gertrude was about to receive Communion, she asked Jesus to offer for her the perfection with which He presented Himself to God the Father at His Ascension. Later she asked Him the effects of her prayer.* Our Lord replied: "It has enabled you to appear before the whole court of Heaven with all the ornaments you have desired. Why should you distrust Me, who am all powerful and all merciful, since there is not one upon the earth who could not clothe his friend in his own ornaments and garments, and thereby make him appear as gloriously attired as himself?" (GG)

*Saint Gertrude inquired of God what would be most for the advantage of an invalid for whom she prayed.* Our Lord replied: "Say two words for her with devotion: First, pray that she may preserve her patience. Second, pray that I may make every moment of suffering serve for her spiritual advancement and for My glory, according [to what] the charity of My paternal heart has ordained from all eternity for her salvation. Know that each time you pray thus, you will increase your merit and that of the sick person. . . ." (GG)

*As Gertrude prayed for a person who had an ardent desire to advance in perfection, she received this instruction:* "Let her often reflect on My mercy, and then on the paternal goodness with which I am ready to relieve men when they have fallen if they return to Me by penance." (GG)

*As the saint ardently desired to have some relics of the wood of the cross so that Our Lord might look on her with more love, He said to her:* "If you desire to have relics which will draw My heart into yours, read My passion and meditate attentively on every word contained in it. It will be for you a true relic that will merit more graces for you than any other." (GG)

*Regarding prayer for the conversion of others, Jesus said:* "First, they must touch them [sinners] gently, and endeavor by their kindness and charitable advice to withdraw them from their imperfections. When they see that these means are ineffectual, then, in the course of time, they may use stronger remedies to effect their cure. Those who care nothing for My words are they who, while they know of the faults of others, concern themselves so little about them that they would not correct them even by a word, for fear of giving themselves the least trouble, saying with Cain, 'Am I my brother's keeper?'" (GG)

*When a Benedictine brother was dying, Saint Gertrude was busy and thus did not pray for him. She felt guilty for this and after he had died she asked the Lord to reward the brother's soul. Jesus said:* "I have rewarded him for his fidelity in three ways, in answer to the prayers of the congregation. From his natural benevolence he took the greatest pleasure in conferring favors on others, and I have renewed in him all this pleasure for each act of kindness which he performed. I have also accumulated in his soul all the gratification and joy which he obtained for others by these acts of benevolence—such as giving a child a toy, a poor person a penny, a sick person some fruit, or any other relief. And lastly, I have made him rejoice exceedingly on account of the approbation which I have manifested for these actions, and I will soon supply all that he needs to attain perfect felicity." (GG)

*Regarding a Mass and prayers that were offered for a deceased person, Jesus said:* "He is not yet so perfectly purified as to be worthy to enjoy My presence, though he is approaching nearer and nearer to this purity by the prayers which are offered for him, and he is more consoled and relieved. His obstinacy in following his own will and his disinclination to submit to the will of others have prevented him from obtaining relief from your prayers as speedily as he would otherwise have done." (GG)

*Saint Margaret Mary entered religious life without knowing how to make mental prayer. Her superior told her to go and place herself before our Lord like a blank canvas before a painter. She wrote:* "As soon as I went to prayer, my sovereign master gave me to understand that the canvas was my soul whereon He wished to paint all the features of His suffering life, which had been spent wholly in love, silence, privation and solitude, and finally had been consummated in sacrifice. These characters He would imprint on my soul after having purified it from all the stains with which it was as yet sullied, both through the love of self and through affection for earthly things and for creatures, to whom my compliant nature was much drawn. At that moment He deprived me of everything, and after having emptied my heart and laid bare my soul, He enkindled in it such an ardent desire to love Him and to suffer that I no longer had any rest. He pursued me so closely that I had no leisure except to think of how I could love Him by crucifying myself. His goodness towards me has ever been so great that He has never failed to provide me with means of doing so." (MMA)

# Providence

"I have delayed answering your prayers because you have not yet sufficient confidence in the effects which My mercy produces in you." (GG)

*Saint Gertrude asked Jesus:* "How is it that My words have so little effect on some persons, notwithstanding the ardent desire I have to lead them to glorify You and to save themselves?" *Our Lord replied:* "Marvel not if your words are sometimes fruitless and produce no effect, since when I dwelt among men My own words, though uttered with the fervor and power of the Godhead, produced not the fruit of salvation in the hearts of all. It is through My divine providence that all things are arranged and perfected in the fitting time, as appointed by me." (GG)

"The kingdom of Heaven cannot be obtained without suffering." (GG)

"When your soul goes forth from your body, I will hide you under My paternal care, as a mother would cover and caress her beloved child when terrified by fear of shipwreck. And as the mother would rejoice in the joy of her child when they had reached land in safety, so will I rejoice in your joy when you are safe in Paradise." (GG)

*Regarding her search to find a suitable building in which to found the Saint Joseph monastery, Saint Teresa of Avila wrote:* "The house struck me as being very small, so small that it didn't seem to be adequate for a monastery; and I wanted to buy another house next to it, which was also small, to serve as the church. I had no means or way of buying this nor did I know what to do. And one day after Communion, the Lord said to me: 'I've already told you to enter as best you can.' And by way of exclamation He added: 'Oh, covetousness of the human race, that you think you will be lacking even ground! How many times did I sleep in the open because I had no place else!' I was astonished and saw that He was right. I went to the little house and drew up plans and found that although small, it was perfect for a monastery, and I didn't bother about buying more property." (TA)

## Purity

*As Gertrude prayed once for a person who ardently desired to have the merit of virginity before God but who feared to have tarnished its brightness by some human weakness . . . Jesus gave this instruction:* "When virginity receives some slight stain through human weakness and this becomes the occasion of exercising a true and solid penance, I cause these stains to appear as ornaments on the soul, and they adorn it as folds adorn a robe." (GG)

"There is no person, however sinful, who may not hope for pardon by offering My passion and death to God My Father, provided that he believes firmly that he will obtain this grace, and that he is persuaded that the memory of My sufferings is the most powerful remedy against sin, when joined to a right faith and true penance." (GG)

"Our Lord warned me once," *Saint Margaret Mary wrote,* "that Satan had asked to try me like gold in the furnace, in the crucible of contradictions and humiliations, of temptations and derelictions, and that He had given him full liberty with the exception of impurity. Having such hatred for that vice,

He would not allow him to trouble me on that score, even as He had never permitted Satan to attack Him in the slightest way in that matter. But as for all other temptations, He said I must be on my guard, especially against those of pride, despair and gluttony, of which I had a greater horror than of death. But He assured me I need fear nothing, as He would be as an impregnable fortress within me, and that He would fight for me and surround me with His power that I might not succumb, and that He himself would be the reward of my victories. But He added that I must continually watch over my exterior." (MMA)

*Whenever Saint Margaret Mary became conscious of a fault, Jesus would come to her assistance and like a good father would stretch out His loving arms towards her and say:* "Now you know full well that you cannot do anything without me." (MMA)

# Reparation

*Saint Gertrude prayed that her monastery might be defended from the threats of adversaries. She received this reply:* "If you humble yourselves under My mighty hand and acknowledge before Me in the secret of your hearts that your sins have merited this chastisement, My paternal mercy will protect you from all the efforts of your enemies. But if you rise up proudly against those who persecute you, wishing them evil for evil, then by My just judgment I will permit them to become stronger than you and to afflict you still more." (GG)

*Saint Gertrude said to Jesus:* "If you acknowledge me as your unworthy servant and accept me as your ambassador, I will gladly announce some special exercise for your love to all who are devoutly disposed, in order to honor you in reparation for the sins now committed." *Our Lord replied:* "Whoever will be My ambassador on this occasion will have this reward: all which he gains for Me will be acquired and gained for himself." (GG)

*Our Lord once appeared to Saint Gertrude tied to a pillar between two executioners, one of whom tore Him with thorns, and the other bruised Him with a whip full of large knots. Both were striking His disfigured face. Saint Gertrude cried out:* "Alas, Lord, what remedy can we find to soothe the agonizing pains of Your divine face?" *Our Lord replied:* "The most efficacious and the tenderest remedy which you can prepare for Me is to meditate lovingly on My passion, and to pray charitably for the conversion of sinners. These two executioners represent the laity, who offend God openly, striking Him with thorns, and the religious, who strike Him still more unpitiably with the knotted cords of secret sins. But both offend Him to the face, and outrage the very God of Heaven." (GG)

"Offer Me all your actions and all that concerns you, in union with the entire submission with which I said these words: 'My Father, Your will be done.' Receive all that happens to you, whether painful or agreeable, with the same love with which I send it to you for your salvation. Be grateful in prosperity, uniting yourself with the love which made Me send it to you. Endure your weakness, that temporal prosperity may lead you to think of spiritual joys and to hope for them. Receive adversity also in union with the charity with which My paternal love sends it to you to prepare you for eternal good." (GG)

"Although the souls of the departed are much benefited by these vigils and other prayers, nevertheless a few words said with affection and devotion are of far more value to them. And this may easier be explained by a familiar comparison, for it is much easier to wash away the stains of mud or dirt from the hands by rubbing them quickly in a little water than by pouring a quantity of water on them without using any friction. Thus, a single word said with fervor and devotion for the souls of the departed is far more efficacious than many vigils and prayers offered coldly and performed negligently." (GG)

"I take particular pleasure in prayers for the dead when they are addressed to Me from a natural compassion united to a good will; thus a good work becomes perfected." (GG)

*On one occasion, while Saint Margaret Mary was praying before the Blessed Sacrament, Jesus presented Himself to her and made known to her to what an excess He had loved men, from whom He received only ingratitude and contempt, telling her:* "I feel this more than all that I suffered during My passion. If only they would make Me some return for My love, I should think but little of all I have done for them and would wish, were it possible, to suffer still more. But the sole return they make for all My eagerness to do them good is to reject Me and treat Me with coldness. You, at least, console Me by supplying for their ingratitude as far as you are able." (MMA)

*Jesus said to Saint Margaret Mary:* "In the first place you shall receive Me in Holy Communion as often as obedience will permit you [and accept] whatever mortification or humiliation it may cause you, which you must take as pledges of My love. You shall, moreover, communicate on the first Friday of each month. Every night between

Thursday and Friday I will make you share in the mortal sadness which I was pleased to feel in the Garden of Olives, and this sadness, without your being able to understand it, shall reduce you to a kind of agony harder to endure than death itself. And in order to bear Me company in the humble prayer that I then offered to My Father in the midst of My anguish, you shall rise between eleven o'clock and midnight and remain prostrate with Me for an hour, not only to appease divine anger by begging mercy for sinners, but also to mitigate in some way the bitterness which I felt at that time on finding Myself abandoned by My apostles, which obliged Me to reproach them for not being able to watch one hour with Me. During that hour you shall do what I shall teach you. But listen, believe not lightly and trust not every spirit, for Satan is enraged and will seek to deceive you. Therefore do nothing without the approval of those who guide you. Being thus under the authority of obedience, his efforts against you will be in vain, for he has no power over the obedient." (MMA)

*Once after Saint Margaret Mary attempted to make reparation for a fault by performing an act so repulsive to nature that no superior would have permitted it, Jesus reprimanded her saying:* "You are indeed foolish to act thus!"

*Margaret replied:* "My divine master, it was in order to please you and to win your Sacred Heart which, I hope, You will not refuse me. But You, O My Lord, what have not You done to win the hearts of men, and yet they refuse them to You and often drive You from them!"

*Jesus responded:* "It is true, My daughter, that My love has made Me sacrifice everything for them, and they make Me no return. But I wish you to supply for their ingratitude by [the] merits of My Divine Heart. I will give you My heart, but you must first constitute your self its holocaust, so that, by its intervention, you may turn aside the chastisements which the divine justice of My Father is about to inflict upon a religious community which in His just wrath He wishes to correct and chastise." (MMA)

"And though I was to do all my actions for him, He willed that His Divine Heart should have a special part in each one. For example, when at recreation, I was to offer Him its share by enduring sufferings, humiliations, mortifications and the rest, with which He would always provide me, and which on that account I was to accept willingly. In like manner in the refectory I was to give up for its satisfaction whatever was most to my taste, and so on with all my other exercises." (MMA)

*Saint Margaret Mary wanted to perform a very austere act of penance in order to make reparation for the insults and dishonor Our Lord receives in the most Holy Sacrament, but before she could do so He forbade her.* "He desired to restore me in perfect health to my superior," *she wrote,* "who had confided and entrusted me to his care. He added that the sacrifice of my desire [to do this penance] would be more agreeable to Him than the fulfillment of it, and that being a Spirit, He desired also sacrifice of the spirit." (MMA)

## Sacred Heart of Jesus

"Whenever you desire to obtain anything from Me, offer Me My heart, which I have so often given you as a token of our mutual friendship, in union with the love which made Me become man for the salvation of men." (GG)

*One day while Saint Margaret Mary was praying before the Blessed Sacrament, Jesus said to her:* "My Divine Heart is so inflamed with love for men, and for you in particular, that being unable any longer to contain within itself the flames of its burning charity, it must spread them abroad by your means, and manifest itself to them [mankind] in order to enrich them with the precious treasures which I discover to you, and which contain graces of sanctification and salvation necessary to withdraw them from the abyss of perdition. I have chosen you as an abyss of unworthiness and ignorance for the accomplishment of this great design, in order that everything may be done by Me." (MMA)

"After allowing her to repose on His Sacred Heart, He [Jesus] asked me [Saint Margaret Mary] for my heart, which I begged Him to take. He did so and placed it in His own heart, where He showed it to me as a little atom which was being consumed in this great furnace, and withdrawing it as a burning flame in the form of a heart, He restored it to the place from where He had taken it, saying to me: 'See, My well-beloved, I give you a precious token of My love, having enclosed within your side a little spark of its glowing flames, that it may serve you for a heart and consume you to the last moment of your life. Its ardor will never be exhausted, and you will be able to find some slight relief only by bleeding. Even this remedy I shall so mark with My cross, that it will bring you more humiliation and suffering than alleviation. Therefore I will that you ask for it with simplicity, both that you may practice what is ordered you as also to give you the consolation of shedding your blood on the cross of humiliations. As a proof that the great favor I have done you is not imagination and that it is the foundation of all those which I intend further to confer upon you, even though I have closed the wound in your side, the pain will always remain. If previously you have taken only the name of My slave, I now give you that of the beloved disciple of My Sacred Heart.'" (MMA)

*After representing her inability to console Him for man's ingratitude, Jesus told Saint Margaret Mary:* "'Behold, this will supply for all that is wanting to you.' And at the same time, His heart being opened, there issued from it a flame so ardent that I thought I should be consumed, for I was wholly penetrated with it, and being no longer able to bear it, I besought Him to have pity on my weakness." (MMA)

*After a night of great humiliation, suffering and torment, Saint Margaret Mary heard Jesus say:* "At last peace is restored, and My sanctity of justice is satisfied by the sacrifice you have made in honor of that which I made at the moment of My incarnation in the womb of My Mother. I wished to renew and unite the merit of it with this act of yours in order to apply it in favor of charity, as I have shown you. So it is that you must no longer lay any claim to whatever they may do or suffer, either to increase your merits or to make satisfaction by penance or otherwise, since everything is sacrificed in favor of charity. Therefore, in imitation of Me, you must act and suffer in silence without any other interest than the glory of God, in the establishment of the reign of My Sacred Heart in the hearts of men, to whom I wish to manifest it by your means." (MMA)

"My sovereign master had promised me [Saint Margaret Mary] shortly after I had consecrated myself to Him, that He would send me one of His servants, to whom He wished to make known according to the knowledge He would give me, all the treasures and secrets of His Sacred Heart which He had confided to me. He added that He sent him to reassure me with regard to my interior way, and that He would impart to him signal graces from His Sacred Heart, showering him abundantly over our interviews. When that holy man [Saint Claude de la Colombiere] came and was addressing the community, I interiorly heard these words: 'This is he whom I send you.'" (MMA)

*One day, after receiving Holy Communion, the Lord showed Saint Margaret Mary His Sacred Heart as a burning furnace, and two other hearts [that of hers and that of her confessor, Saint Claude de la Colombiere, S.J.] that were on the point of uniting themselves to it, and of being absorbed in it. At the point of their hearts being absorbed into His, He said to her:* "It is thus My pure love unites these three hearts forever." *Our Lord afterwards revealed to Saint Margaret Mary that this union was all for the glory of His Sacred Heart, the treasure of which He wished her to reveal to Father de la Colombiere, that he might spread devotion to it, and make known to others their value and utility. He wished Margaret and this holy priest to be as brother and sister, sharing equally these spiritual treasures. Saint Margaret Mary objected, showing Jesus her poverty and the inequality which existed between a man of such great virtue and merit [Father de la Colombiere] and herself, but Jesus replied:* "The infinite riches of My heart will supply for and equalize everything. Tell him this without fear." (MMA)

"On one occasion my sovereign sacrificer asked me [Saint Margaret Mary] to make in His favor and in writing a will or an entire and unreserved donation, as I had already done verbally, of all that I should do and suffer, and of all the prayers and spiritual goods which should be offered for me, either during my life or after my death. . . . When I presented the testament to this only love of my soul, He expressed great pleasure, and said that He wished to dispose of it according to His design and in favor of whomever He pleased. His love having despoiled me of everything, He did not wish me to have other riches than those of His Sacred Heart, of which He there and then made me a donation. He told me to write it in my blood according as He dictated it to me. I then signed it on my heart, writing thereon the sacred name of Jesus with a penknife. He then said that since I no longer had any claim to the good done to me, He would not fail to reward it a hundredfold, as though it were done to Himself." (MMA)

"On one occasion, my sovereign Lord gave me [Saint Margaret Mary] to understand that He wished to withdraw me into solitude, not into the solitude of the desert, but into that of His Sacred Heart, where He wished to honor me with His most familiar converse like that of friend with friend. There He would give me further instructions regarding His will and would renew my strength to enable me to fulfill it and to fight courageously until death, for I had still to sustain the attacks of several powerful enemies." (MMA)

*While showing Saint Margaret Mary His Sacred Heart, Jesus said:* "Behold this heart, which has loved men so much that it has spared nothing, even to exhausting and consuming itself, in order to testify to them its love. In return I receive from the greater number nothing but ingratitude by reason of their irreverence and sacrileges, and by the coldness and contempt which they show Me in this sacrament of love. But what I feel the most keenly is that it is hearts which are consecrated to Me that treat Me thus. Therefore, I ask of you that the Friday after [the] Octave of Corpus Christi be set apart for a special feast to honor My heart, by communicating on that day and making reparation to it by a solemn act, in order to make amends for the indignities which it has received during the time it has been exposed on the altars. I promise you that My heart shall expand itself to shed upon those who shall thus honor it and cause it to be honored." (MMA)

*Once when Saint Margaret Mary was doing work on her knees, the heart of Jesus appeared to her, brighter than the sun. It was surrounded by the flames of its pure love and encircled by seraphim, who sang in marvelous harmony:* "Love triumphs, love enjoys! The love of the Sacred Heart rejoices!" *These blessed spirits invited her to unite with them in praising this Divine Heart, but Margaret Mary did not dare do so. They reproved her, she wrote, telling her* "they had come in order to form an association with me, whereby to render it a perpetual homage of love, adoration and praise, and that for this purpose they would take my place before the Blessed Sacrament. Thus I might be able, by their means, to love continually, and, as they would participate in my love and suffer in my person, I on my part, should rejoice in and with them." (MMA)

## Scripture

"Once while in prayer the delight I felt within me was so great that, as someone who is unworthy of such good, I began to think about how I merited rather to be in that place I had seen was reserved for me in Hell . . . there came upon me a spiritual rapture that I don't know how to describe . . . I was told without seeing anyone, but I clearly understood that it was Truth itself telling me: 'This is no small thing I do for you, because it is one of the things for which you owe Me a great deal; for all the harm that comes to the world comes from its not knowing the truths of Scripture in clarity and truth. Not one iota of Scripture will fall short.'" (TA)

"I thought that [other peoples' recommendations to pray rather than found monasteries] would be God's will because of what Saint Paul said about the enclosure of women. . . . The Lord said to me: 'Tell them they shouldn't follow just one part of Scripture but that they should look at other parts, and ask them if they can by chance tie my hands.'"(TA)

"As I am the Salvation and life of the soul, and as I continually hunger and thirst for the salvation of men, if you endeavor to study some words of Scripture every day for the benefit of others, you will bestow on Me a most sweet reflection." (GG)

## Spiritual Life—What Pleases God

"The fidelity that moves My heart consists in persons [performing] their duty when they find themselves in good health, and immediately desisting and entrusting all to Me when they find themselves indisposed." (GG)

"A good king never takes it ill of his queen if she neglects bringing forward at a given hour the ornaments that he is most gratified at receiving, but he is much more pleased at finding her always ready to comply with his wishes. The sweetness of My most benign Heart delights more in the patient endurance with which My chosen one bears her infirmity." (GG)

*Saint Gertrude asked the Lord why one of the sisters had been fearful during her death agony:* "I was hidden on her left side, [but] as soon as she was sufficiently purified, I showed

Myself to her, and took her with Me to eternal rest and glory." (GG)

"A bridegroom admires the personal beauty of his bride more than her ornaments, and in like manner I prefer the virtue of humility to the grace of devotion." (GG)

*As Gertrude saw one of her sisters approaching the Holy Eucharist with extreme emotions of fear, she turned from her with a feeling of indignation. But the Lord charitably reproved her by these words:* "Do you not know that I am honored by reverence as well as by love? But human weakness is not able to combine the two at one moment, and all are the members of one body. Those who have less should take from those who have more. For example, let she who is more moved by the sweetness of My love think less of the duty of respect, and be thankful that another supplies for her deficiency by being more exact in testifying her reverence. Let the other one desire to obtain the joy and consolation that another soul possesses." (GG)

"I would [prefer] that My elect not consider Me so severe, but rather believe that I should receive as a benefit the least service they render Me at their own expense." (GG)

*As the Saint prayed for a person who had abstained from receiving the Body of the Lord, fearing to be an occasion of scandal, Our Lord made known His will by this comparison:* "As a man who washes his hands to remove a stain, removes at the same time not only what he has seen but also cleanses his hands perfectly, so the just are allowed to fall into some trifling faults, that they may become more agreeable to Me by their repentance and humility." (GG)

*Our Lord told Saint Gertrude how to learn patience:*
"Consider how a king honors those who are most like him
with his friendship, and learn from this how the love which
I bear you is increased when, for love of Me, you suffer contempt like I endured. Secondly, consider how much the court
respects he who is most like the king and is most intimate
with him. This same glory is prepared for you in Heaven as
the reward of your patience. Thirdly, consider what consolation the tender compassion of a faithful friend gives to his
friend, and learn from this what compassion I feel in Heaven
for even the least thought which afflicts you here." (GG)

*The saint inquired:* "How, Lord, do You receive the special devotion which some have for the image of Your cross?"
*Our Lord replied:* "It is very acceptable to Me. Nevertheless,
when those who have a special devotion to these representa-
tions of My cross fail to imitate the example of My passion,
their conduct is like that of a mother who, to gratify herself
and for her own honor, adorns her daughter with different
ornaments but refuses her harshly what she most desires
to have. While this mother deprives her child of what she
wishes for, the child cares little for all else that is given to her,
because she knows it is done through pride and not from
affection. So all the testimonies of love, respect and reverence
that are offered to the image of My cross will not be perfectly
acceptable to Me unless the examples of My passion are also
imitated." (GG)

"If a master, when questioned by people who speak different languages, answered each in the one tongue, his discourse
would only profit those who understood it. But if he speaks
to each in his own tongue—in Latin to him who understands
Latin and in Greek to him who understands Greek—then

each can comprehend what is said. Thus the greater the diversity with which I communicate my gifts, the more my impenetrable wisdom is displayed which replies to each according to their comprehension and the understanding with which I have gifted them—speaking to the simple by plain and sensible parables and to the enlightened in a more sublime and hidden manner." (GG)

"Even as an avaricious person would be sorry to lose the opportunity of gaining a single penny, so I, who find all My joy in you, do not intend to allow even your least thought nor a single movement of your finger, which you have done for love of Me, to pass by without using it for My glory and your eternal welfare." (GG)

"If anyone desires that her zeal [for the conversion of sinners] should be an acceptable sacrifice to Me and useful to her own soul, she should have a special care of three things. First, she should show a gentle and serene countenance toward those whom she desires to correct for their faults, and even, when opportunity offers, she should manifest her charity toward them by her actions as well as by her words. Second, she should be careful not to communicate these faults in places where she neither expects amendment in the person corrected nor caution in the listeners. Third, when her conscience urges her to reprehend any fault, no human consideration should induce her to be silent, but from a pure motive of giving glory to God and benefiting souls, let her seek an opportunity of correcting these imperfections with profit and charity. Then she will be rewarded according to her labor, not according to her success, for if her care entirely fails in effect, it will not be her fault but the fault of those who refuse to hear her." (GG)

"O Eternal Wisdom," *asked Saint Gertrude,* "since You foresaw all the excesses and crimes that we do, why did You promise that You would not again destroy the world by a flood?" *Jesus replied:* "I made it [the promise] to strengthen them in their good resolutions during the calm of prosperity, so that in the storm of affliction they may be bound in honor to keep their promise." (GG)

*On the Tuesday before Ash Wednesday, a day on which people in the world commit the greatest excesses in eating and drinking, Saint Gertrude heard the bell ringing for the workmen's breakfast, and exclaimed with a sigh:* "Alas My Lord, how early in the day men begin to offend You by their gourmandizing!" *But Our Lord replied:* "Do not grieve, My beloved. Those who are now summoned to the meal are not of the number of those who offend Me by greediness, since this reflection is a warning to them to apply to work, and I take as much satisfaction in seeing them eat as a man would seeing his horse refreshed when he needed its labor." (GG)

"If you read with the intention of obtaining the grace of compunction or devotion, you appease My thirst by giving Me an agreeable beverage to drink. If you employ yourself in recollection for an hour each day, you give Me hospitality; and if you apply yourself daily to acquire some new virtue, you clothe me. You visit Me when sick by striving to overcome temptation and to conquer your evil inclinations, and you visit Me in prison and solace My afflictions with the sweetest consolations, when you pray for sinners and for the souls in Purgatory." (GG)

"Those who perform these devotions daily for My love, especially during the holy season of Lent, will most certainly receive the tenderest and most beautiful recompense which My incomprehensible omnipotence, My inscrutable wisdom, and My most loving benevolence can bestow." (GG)

"Cast from you all the vices which you desire should die in you, and draw into you, by the virtue of My Spirit, those perfections of Mine which you desire to possess. Be assured that your sins will be pardoned and that you shall feel the salutary effects of what you have thus drawn from Me into yourself." (GG)

"He who follows the will of another and not his own, frees Me from the captivity which I endured when bound with chains on the morning of My passion. He who considers himself guilty satisfies for My condemnation by false witnesses. He who renounces the pleasures of sense consoles Me for the blows which I received. He who submits to pastors who try him consoles Me for the crowning with thorns. He who humbles himself first in a dispute carries My cross. He who performs works of charity consoles Me when My limbs were cruelly fastened to the cross. He who spares himself neither pain nor labor to withdraw his neighbor from sin consoles Me for My death for the salvation of the human race. He who replies gently when reproached takes Me down from the cross. Lastly, he who prefers his neighbor to himself lays Me in the sepulcher." (GG)

"The good and praiseworthy custom which you have of recommending your actions to Me so frequently and of placing them in My hands, makes Me correct those which are defective so that they may please Me perfectly and all My celestial court." (GG)

"In order that sensible things may assist you to understand those which are spiritual, consider that a bridegroom finds the greatest pleasure in the most familiar relations with his bride. I assure you that no bridegroom ever found more satisfaction in the endearments of his bride than I do whenever My elect offer Me their hearts, purified from all sin, that I may take My delight in them." (GG)

*During Mass one day, Our Lord gave Saint Gertrude this instruction:* "Consider the example I give to My elect in honoring this cross, and know that I honored the instruments of My passion, which caused Me suffering, more than those things which in My infancy were used for My convenience. If you desire to imitate My example and to give Me glory and further your own salvation, you will love your enemies more than your friends, and this will advance you marvelously in perfection. The reason I so specially loved this cross was that I obtained through it the redemption of mankind, which I so ardently desired, even as devout persons love the times and places where they have received special favors from God." (GG)

"Whoever observes the regular [six-month] fast because of zeal for religious observance and purely for My love, and who seeks not his own advantage but Mine, I will accept it from him. . . . But if obedience and necessity obliges him to relax his fast against his will, and he submits in union with the humility with which I submitted to men when on earth for the glory of My Father, I will treat him as a friend would his dearest friend whom he had invited to his table." (GG)

"Now I, your Lord and your God, am the true and faithful lover of your soul; and I share in all the pains of body or soul with which you are afflicted, and send My saints to attend you and congratulate you on this royal road which leads you to Me. The instruments of music and rejoicing [that I hear] are your sufferings which resound in My ears as a harmonious concert, moving Me to pity you and to incline My Heart more and more toward you. Then, when you arrive at your journey's end, I will meet you and espouse you before all My saints with a holy embrace in the Sacrament of Extreme Unction. The sooner you receive this sacrament, the greater will be your happiness, for then I will approach you nearer and nearer so that your whole being will be enraptured with the blessedness of My embrace; and I will convey you myself across the dark river death, immersing you in the ocean of My divinity, where you will become one spirit with Me and reign with Me for endless ages." (GG)

*Regarding souls who wish for the grace of a happy death, Jesus said:* "If anyone desires a similar visit in his last moments, let him endeavor daily to clothe himself with My perfect life and to imitate it continually. Let him learn to subdue his flesh and to renounce his own will entirely into My hands. Let him live by the Spirit and believe that I will seek his good in all things by My paternal providence. Let him offer Me every adversity and contradiction, and for each I will reward him with rich jewels and precious gifts. If through human frailty he seeks himself in anything, let him immediately do penance and once more resign himself to My will, and I will receive him with the right hand of My mercy and lead him with ineffable honor and glory to the kingdom of eternal light." (GG)

## Spiritual Life—Cooperating with God

"I have no other joy," *Saint Gertrude prayed,* "than to desire that Your amiable and peaceful will may always be accomplished in Me and in all creatures, and I am ready, for this end, to offer every member of my body to be exposed one after the other to the acutest suffering." *The Lord replied:* "Since you have desired with such ardor to see the designs of My will executed, I will reward you with this recompense, that you shall appear as agreeable in My eyes as if you had never violated My will, even in the most trifling matter." (GG)

"When, moved by My love, I visit one of the faithful in the Sacrament of the Altar, all who are in Heaven, on earth or in Purgatory receive immense benefits from it." (GG)

*When Saint Gertrude desired death in order to be united to Our Lord, she heard these words:* "Whenever anyone desires with all their heart to be delivered from the prison of the body, and yet, at the same time, is perfectly willing to remain there so long as it shall please God, Jesus Christ unites the merit of His adorable life to theirs, which renders them marvelously perfect in the sight of the Eternal Father." (GG)

"Those who endeavor to turn their minds from all which they know to be displeasing to Me, and who endeavor to please Me in all things, shall receive the light of My Divine Heart to direct their thoughts." (GG)

"The virtue of concord [harmony] is not injured when men oppose injustice." (GG)

"One day, after Communion, He [Jesus] showed me [Saint Margaret Mary], if I am not mistaken, that He was the most beautiful, the wealthiest, the most powerful, the most perfect and the most accomplished amongst all lovers. After having pledged myself to Him for so many years, how came it, He said, that I now sought to break with Him for another?" *Jesus said:* "Oh! Be assured that if you do Me this wrong, I will abandon you forever. But if you remain faithful to Me, I will never leave you. I Myself will be your victory over all your enemies. I pardon your ignorance because as yet, you do not know Me. But if you are faithful to Me and follow Me, I will teach you to know Me, and I will manifest Myself to you." (MMA)

*Saint Margaret Mary heard the following words:* "Nothing is sullied in innocence, nothing is lost in power; nothing passes away in this blessed abode. There, all is made perfect in love." *Sometime later regarding this experience, she wrote:* "The explanation of these words served me a long time as a matter for meditation. 'Nothing is sullied in innocence'—that is to say, I was not to allow any stain to remain in my soul or in my heart. 'Nothing is lost in power'—by this I understood that I was to give and abandon everything to Him, who is power itself, and that one loses nothing by giving Him all. The other two lines referred to paradise, where nothing passes away, for everything there is lasting and is consummated in love. A slight glimpse of that glory was then revealed to me, and, O God! Into what a transport of joy and desire did it now throw me!" (MMA)

"When He desired something from me [Saint Margaret Mary], He urged me so strongly that it was impossible for me to resist. This was a cause of much suffering to me, for I was often inclined to resist, as He took me by all that was most opposed to my nature and inclinations and wished that I should unceasingly act contrary to them." (MMA)

# Spiritual Life—Hindrances and Evils

*One day, when a sister abstained from Communion without any reasonable cause, Jesus said:* "What can I do for her, since she has herself so covered her eyes with the veil of her unworthiness that she cannot possibly see the tenderness of My paternal Heart?" (GG)

"I will never permit My elect to be tried beyond their strength, and I am always with them to moderate the burden of their adversity. . . . When I know that it is necessary to purify My elect by sufferings, I send them not for their destruction, but to prove them and to contribute to their salvation." (GG)

"Make each of these words which annoy you an ornament of virtue [by patiently enduring them], and then come to Me, and I will be moved by My goodness and receive you lovingly. The more you are blamed, the more My Heart will incline towards you, since you thus become more like Me, for I suffered contradictions continually." (GG)

"In My infinite and ever-active love, I continually go forth in search of souls in order to guide them to life eternal, and illuminating them with My light, I move the free-will of men in many and diverse ways. When man yields to My inspirations, I increase this light, and by its aid he sees himself imprisoned, as it were, in a foul and dismal den surrounded by a brood of venomous reptiles which strive to destroy him but which he did not see before by reason of the darkness. . . ." (CoG)

"I move with My love the heart of man, and with that movement give him light by which he sees that I am inspiring him to well-doing. In that light he ceases to do ill and struggles with his evil inclinations." (CoG)

"What do you fear? Can a child loved as much as I love you perish in the arms of a Father who is omnipotent?" (MMA)

"After Holy Communion He asked me [Saint Margaret Mary] to renew the sacrifice I had already made Him of my liberty and of my whole being, and I did so with all my heart. 'Provided, O Sovereign Master!' I said, 'that You will never allow anything extraordinary to appear in me, but what may cause me humiliation and abjection before creatures and lower me in their esteem. For, alas! O my God, I feel my weakness, I fear to betray You, and that Your gifts should not be in safety with me!'"

*Jesus replied:* "Fear nothing My daughter. Leave all to Me, for I will constitute Myself the guardian of them and render you powerless to resist Me." (MMA)

*"Thus He told me and wanted me to see clearly that He was always present in conversations like these [i.e. conversations with others about God] and how much He is pleased when persons so delight in speaking of Him."* (TA)

# Suffering I

*Our Lord appeared to Saint Gertrude, bearing on His sacred shoulders a vast magnificent building, and said:* "Behold with what labor, care, and vigilance I carry this beloved house, which is none other than that of religion. It is everywhere threatened with ruin, because there are so few who are willing to do or to suffer anything for its support and increase. You, therefore, should suffer with Me in bearing it; for all those who endeavor by their words or actions to extend religion and who try to establish it in its first fervor and purity, are so many strong pillars which sustain this holy house and comfort Me by sharing with Me the weight of this burden." (GG)

"When I take pleasure in displaying the beauty of My chosen one in the presence of the ever-adorable Trinity and the heavenly host, I oppress her with sickness and infirmity." (GG)

"Whoever offers himself willingly to suffer anything in order to please Me, he truly glorifies Me, and, glorifying Me, tells Me that he languishes for love of Me, provided that he continues patiently, and that he never turns his eyes away from Me. . . . The unction of My love is so powerfully moved [by those who willingly suffer for Jesus] that I am compelled to heal the contrite heart—that is to say, those who desire this grace; to preach to those who are in captivity—that is, to pardon sinners; to open the door to those who are in prison— that is, to release the souls in Purgatory." (GG)

*As Saint Gertrude felt an illness coming on her immediately before a feast day, she desired that Our Lord would preserve her health until it was over, or at least permit her to have sufficient strength to assist at it. Even so, she abandoned herself entirely to the will of God. Then she received this reply from the Lord:* "In asking Me these things and at the same time in submitting entirely to My will, you lead Me into a garden of delights enameled with flowers, which is most agreeable to Me. I know that if I grant what you ask and allow you to assist at these services, I shall be obliged to follow you into the place which pleases you. But if I refuse you this and you still continue patiently, you will follow Me into the place which I prefer, because I find more pleasure in you in a state of suffering than if you have devotion accompanied by pleasure." (GG)

*Gertrude said to the Lord:* "Father of mercies! After this sickness, which is the seventh that I have had, will you restore me to my former health?" *Our Lord replied:* "If I had made known to you at the commencement of your first illness that you would have to endure seven, perhaps you would have given way to impatience through human frailty. So also if I now promised you that this would be the last sickness, the hope with which you would look forward to its termination might lesson your merit. Therefore the paternal providence of My uncreated wisdom has wisely ordained that you should remain ignorant on both subjects, that you might be obliged to have recourse to Me continually with your whole heart and to commend your troubles, whether exterior or interior, to My fidelity." (GG)

*Saint Gertrude prayed for some people who were undergoing hardships, noting that they deserved better rewards than she had received from God.* The Lord told her: "In these things as in all others, I manifest the special charity and tenderness which I have for you; even as a mother who loves her only child wishes to adorn her with ornaments of gold and silver, but knowing that she could not bear their weight, decks her with different flowers, which without disturbing her, do not fail to add to her attractions. So also I moderate the rigor of your sufferings, lest you should fall under the burden [of them] and thereby be deprived of the merit of patience." (GG)

"If you desire to soothe My pains, you must bear your own." (GG)

*Once, when Saint Gertrude was contemplating Jesus' crown of thorns, His scourging at the pillar, His weariness and the carrying of the cross, she said,* "Behold my sweetest Love, I offer You my heart, desiring to suffer all the bitterness and anguish of Your dear heart, in return for Your love in bearing the undeserved torments of Your passion, and I beseech You that whenever I forget this offering through human frailty to send me some sharp bodily pain which may resemble Yours." *Jesus replied:* "Your desires are sufficient. But if you wish Me to have unbounded pleasure in your heart, let Me act as I please within it, and do not desire that I should give you either consolation or suffering." (GG)

"As a church is secured with locks to prevent the entrance of the unworthy, so I by infirmity seal her [a sick person] up so that her mind cannot be occupied by externals, which tend to disturb the heart and distract it from Me, and in which there is sometimes no great utility." (GG)

*As Saint Gertrude beheld a suffering sister, she said to Our Lord,* "Why has this soul been tormented so painfully, when You are all powerful?" *He replied:* "She has not been tormented, but has waited with joy for the consummation of her happiness, even as a young girl would wait for a festival on which she was to be adorned with the ornaments which her mother had prepared for her." (GG)

*The Blessed Virgin Mary told Saint Gertrude:* "As you never remember to have endured more severe corporal sufferings than those caused by your illness, know also that you have never received from My Son more noble gifts than those which will now be given to you and for which your sufferings have prepared you. . . . This sickness which you suffer will sanctify your soul . . ." (GG)

*Towards evening, as Saint Gertrude was worn out by acute suffering, she sought to obtain some mitigation of it from Our Lord, but He raised His right arm, and showed her the pain she had endured all day as a precious ornament on His bosom. As this ornament appeared so perfect and so complete in every part, she rejoiced, hoping that her suffering would now cease, but Our Lord replied:* "What you suffer after this will add brightness to this ornament." (GG)

*Jesus told Saint Gertrude that one should never attribute his or her own sufferings to the people that make them suffer. He refers to this second group as* "those whom I should make use of to purify [you]." "Rather," *He said regarding those who suffer,* "let them cast their eyes on My paternal love, which would not allow even a breath of wind to approach them unless it furthered their eternal salvation; and therefore they should have compassion on those who stain themselves to purify them." (GG)

"Our Lord," *wrote Saint Gertrude,* "prefers suffering without devotion to devotion without suffering." (GG)

"When those persons whom I have determined to sanctify by suffering seek bodily comforts while they are awake, and thus deprive themselves of occasions of merit, I, in My love, send them sufferings during their sleep so that they may have an opportunity of acquiring merit." (GG)

"Whoever hides his sufferings and adversities in the bouquet of My passion, and joins them to [those] of My sufferings [which] they seem most to resemble, he truly reposes in My bosom, and I will give him, to augment his merits, all that My singular charity has merited by My patience and by My other virtues." (GG)

"In guiding the consciences of My elect, I only let them see temporal advantages to a small extent, in order to avoid exposing their weakness to great temptation and to inspire them more easily with contempt for the false pleasures of the earth." (GG)

"If I thought I could not assist [someone undergoing temptations], My Heart would be so desolate that even all the joys of Heaven could not alleviate My grief, because he is a part of My Body and is united to My divinity. I am ever the advocate of My elect, full of compassion for their every need." (GG)

*On a fast day, when Saint Gertrude was unable to chant due to severe indisposition and headaches, she inquired of God why He so often permitted these infirmities to visit her on festivals. Our Lord replied:* "It is to prevent you from dissipating yourself [being attracted to pleasure to the point of harm] by the pleasures of the harmony of the chant, and so being less disposed to receive grace." "But," *she inquired,* "could not your grace prevent this misfortune?" *To this Our Lord answered:* "It is a greater advantage to men to turn away occasions of falls by trials, because then they have a double-merit: that of patience and that of humility." (GG)

*Once Saint Gertrude exclaimed with ardor,* "O my Savior! Why have I not found a fire sufficiently strong to melt my heart, so that I might pour it forth entirely into You?" "Your will," *replied the Lord,* "will be to you the fire which you desire." *And from this she knew that by the effort of his will man may fully accomplish all that he desires to do for the glory of God.* (GG)

"I am accustomed to afflict those who are dearest to Me with corporal infirmities, with mental depression and other trials, so that when they desire the goods which are opposed to these evils, the ardent love of My heart may reward them with greater profusion." (GG)

"The patience with which anyone endures an evil for My love and for My glory, which cannot be remedied by any human means, is not a patience which I condemn. On the contrary . . . it becomes of incomparable merit and value." (GG)

*As Gertrude prayed for a person who was greatly tried by temptation, she received this reply:* "It is I who have sent this temptation and who permit it, that she may thus perceive and repent of her defects and efface those defects which she does not see. It usually happens that when men perceive any stain on their hands, they wash them, and thus thoroughly cleanse away lesser stains which they would not have perceived or removed if they had not seen a greater one." (GG)

# Suffering II

"My divine master urged me [Saint Margaret Mary] so powerfully to leave all and to follow Him that I no longer had any rest. He also inspired me with so ardent a desire to conform myself to His suffering life that all I endured seemed to be as nothing. This made me redouble my penances, and, prostrating myself at times at the foot of my crucifix, I said: 'How happy should I be, O my dear Savior, if You would imprint on me the likeness of Your sufferings!' To which He replied: 'This is what I intend to do, provided that you do not resist Me and that you on your side contribute.'" (MMA)

"He [Jesus] revealed to me [Saint Margaret Mary] two sanctities in Him, the one of love and the other of justice, both rigorous in their degree, which would continually be brought to bear upon me. The former would make me suffer a most painful kind of Purgatory, in order to relieve the holy souls therein detained whom, according to His good pleasure, He would permit to address themselves to me. And as for His sanctity of justice, which is so terrible to sinners, it would make me feel the weight of His just rigor by causing me to suffer for sinners, and especially, He said, 'for souls consecrated to Me, regarding whom I will in future make you see and feel what you must suffer for love of Me.'" (MMA)

*After experiencing joyful consolations, Saint Margaret Mary asked God if He would always let her live without suffering. A large cross covered with flowers appeared and He replied:* "Behold the bed of My chaste spouses on which I shall make you taste all the delights of My pure love. Little by little these flowers will drop off, and nothing will remain but the thorns, which were hidden because of your weakness. Nevertheless, you shall feel the pricks of these thorns so keenly that you will need all the strength of My love to bear the pain." (MMA)

*Saint Margaret Mary received a deep understanding of the mystery of Jesus' sacred passion and death. She refrained from writing about it except to say:* "It has given me such an intense love of the cross that I cannot live a moment without suffering, but suffering in silence, without consolation, alleviation or compassion, and, in fine, dying with the sovereign of my soul, overwhelmed by the cross of every kind of opprobrium, of sorrow and of humiliation, forgotten and despised by all. This has lasted all my life, which through His mercy has been entirely spent in this manner which is that of pure love, and He has always taken care to provide me with these delicacies, so delicious to His taste, that He never says: 'It is sufficient.'" (MMA)

*The Three Persons of the Trinity presented themselves to Saint Margaret Mary, and it seemed to her the eternal Father presented her with a very heavy cross beset with thorns and surrounded with various instruments of the passion. He said:* "See, My daughter, I make you the same present which I made to My beloved Son." *Our Lord Jesus Christ then said:* "I will fasten you to the cross as I Myself was fastened to it and will bear you faithful company." *The Third Person [The Holy Spirit] then said that* "being love itself, He would purify and consume her on it." (MMA)

*After receiving a glimpse of Heaven, Saint Margaret Mary believed that she was to go there at once and enjoy it, but realized she was mistaken when she was told:*
"In vain your longing heart desires to find an entrance there.
Who to this heavenly bliss aspires, on earth the cross must bear." (MMA)

*Jesus appeared to Saint Margaret Mary holding two pictures—one depicting a religious life of peace spent in the enjoyment of interior and exterior consolation, and the other of suffering in mind and body. He asked her:* "Choose, My daughter, the one which pleases you best. I will give you the same graces with one as with the other." *After telling Him that she would be content with whatever choice He preferred, Jesus presented her with the picture of crucifixion and said:* "Behold what I have chosen for you; that is which is the most agreeable to Me, both in order to accomplish My designs and to render you conformable to Me. The other [the life of consolation] is a life of enjoyment, not of merit." (MMA)

"I [Saint Margaret Mary] felt unalterable peace in the acceptance of all I had to suffer, or would yet have to suffer, as was shown me up to the day of judgment if it were the will of God. Indeed, He willed that I should appear no longer but as an object of contradiction, a very sink of vileness, of contempt and of humiliation which I beheld with pleasure overwhelming me on all sides, and that without any consolation, either human or divine." (MMA)

*At the direction of, and in obedience to her superior, while receiving Holy Communion, Saint Margaret Mary asked the Lord to restore her to health. He said to her:* "Yes, My daughter, I come to you as a sovereign sacrificer to give you renewed vigor in order to immolate you to fresh sufferings." (MMA)

*Some of the sisters in her community thought that Saint Margaret Mary was possessed or obsessed by the devil. They threw holy water at her and made the sign of the cross and other prayers in an unsuccessful attempt to drive away the demon. But Jesus, far from taking flight, drew her even more powerfully to Himself, saying:* "I love holy water, and I have so great an affection for the cross that I cannot refrain from uniting Myself closely with those who bear it like Me, and for the love of Me." (MMA)

*In the midst of believing that she was an object of aversion
to others, that they had great difficulty in bearing with her, that
they looked upon her as a visionary and as clinging obstinately
to her illusions and imagination, Saint Margaret Mary was
not permitted to seek the least alleviation and consolation. Jesus
would not allow it, desiring that she suffer all in silence and take
the following as her motto:*

"In silence shall my suffering be,
pure love from fear my soul does free." (MMA)


"I do you a great honor, My dear daughter, in making use
of such noble instruments to crucify you. My eternal Father
delivered Me to be crucified into the hands of pitiless executioners, but in your regard I make use of souls who are devoted
and consecrated to Me, for the salvation of whom I wish you
to endure all that they will cause you to suffer." (MMA)


*Saint Margaret Mary wrote that Jesus* "wished me to be in
a continual state of sacrifice. To this end, He said He would
increase my sensitiveness and repugnance so that I should
not be able to do anything except with difficulty and great
effort. This was in order to provide me with matter for self-
conquest even in the most trivial and indifferent things. . . .
He added that I should no longer taste any sweetness except
in the bitterness of Calvary, since He would make me find
a martyrdom of all those things in which others find joy,
delight, and temporal happiness." (MMA)


*Once as Saint Margaret Mary was approaching Commu-
nion, the Sacred Host appeared to her shining like the sun, the
brilliancy of which was more than she could bear. In the midst
of it, she beheld Our Lord holding a crown of thorns which He
placed upon her head shortly after she had received Him, saying*

*at the same time:* "Receive this crown, My daughter, as a sign of that which will soon be given you in order to make you conformable to Me." (MMA)

*Jesus appeared to Saint Margaret Mary after Holy Communion as the scourged Christ, laden with His cross, covered with wounds and gashes, His blood flowing on all sides. He said to her in a sorrowful voice full of anguish:* "Is there no one to take pity on Me and share My sorrow in the pitiful state to which sinners reduce Me, especially at the present time?" *Saint Margaret Mary wrote:* "Prostrating myself with tears and groans at His sacred feet, I offered myself to Him, and taking on my shoulders that heavy cross all studded with nails, I was overwhelmed with its weight. I then understood better the grievousness and malice of sin, for which I felt such a horror that I would have preferred a thousand times to cast myself into Hell than to commit a single one willfully." (MMA)

*Jesus revealed one day to Saint Margaret Mary that it was not enough for her to carry the cross, but that she must fasten herself to it with Him in order to keep Him faithful company by sharing in the sufferings, contempt, opprobrium and other indignities of which He was the victim.* (MMA)

"Do you think, daughter, that merit lies in enjoyment? No, rather it lies in working and suffering and loving. Haven't you heard that Saint Paul rejoiced in heavenly joys only once and that he suffered often? Look at My whole life filled with suffering, and only in the incident on Mount Tabor do you hear about My joy. When you see My Mother holding Me in her arms, don't think she enjoyed those consolations without heavy torment. From the time Simeon spoke those words to her, My Father gave her clear light to see what I was to suffer. The great saints who lived in deserts, since they were guided by God, performed severe penances, and besides this, they waged great battle with the devil and with themselves. They spent long periods without any spiritual consolation. Believe, daughter, that My Father gives greater trials to anyone whom He loves more, and love responds to these. How can I show you greater love than by desiring for you what I have desired for Myself? Behold these wounds, for your sufferings have never reached this point. Suffering is the way of truth. By this means you will help Me weep over the loss of those who follow the way of the world, and you will understand that all your desires, cares and thoughts must be employed in how to do the opposite." (TA)

"Having spoken one day to a person who had given up a great deal for God and recalling how I had never given up anything for Him—nor have I ever served Him in accordance with my obligation—and considering the many favors He had bestowed on my soul, I began to grow very anxious. And the Lord said: 'You already know of the espousal between you and Me. Because of this espousal, whatever I have is yours. So I give you all the trials and sufferings I underwent, and by these means, as with something belonging to you, you can make requests of My Father.' Although I had heard we share these, now I had heard it in such a different way that it seemed I felt great dominion. The friendship in which this favor was granted me cannot be described here. It seemed the Father accepted the fact of this sharing; and since then I look very differently upon what the Lord suffered, as something belonging to me—and it gives me great comfort." (TA)

"The cause of all the suffering through which you have to pass is better understood by experience than by reasoning. Yet know this: I make of the body a Purgatory for the soul, and thus augment her glory by drawing her to Me through this Purgatory alone. And thus I am ever knocking at the door of the heart, and if man yields consent and opens to Me, I lead him with continual and loving care to that degree of glory for which I created him. If he could see and understand the care with which I promote his salvation and his welfare . . . even were the universe at his command, he would abandon himself without reserve to Me." (CoG)

## Trust

"I was wondering whether I was to be helpful to others but on account of my sins be lost myself. He said to me: 'Have no fear.'" (TA)

*During a great period of trial, Saint Teresa heard the following words which brought her great peace:* "Do not fear, daughter, for I Am, and I will not abandon you. Do not fear." *Following this, she wrote,* "Behold by these words alone I was given calm together with fortitude, courage, security, quietude and light so that in one moment I saw my soul become another. . . . Oh, what a good God! Oh, how good a Lord and how powerful! He provides not only the counsel but also the remedy! His words are works. . . ." (TA)

"And while I was feeling really desolate, the Lord said to me: 'Don't you know that I am mighty? What do you fear?'" (TA)

"Once while very disturbed and troubled, unable to recollect myself and in battle and strife with my own thoughts which were turning to imperfect matters—finding that I didn't have the detachment I usually do—I feared, since I saw I was so wretched, that the favors the Lord had granted me had been illusions. I experienced, in sum, a great darkness of soul. While I was in this affliction, the Lord began to speak to me. He told me not to be anxious, that in seeing myself in this condition I would understand how miserable I'd be if He withdrew from me, and that there is no security while we live in this flesh. He made me understand how worthwhile this war and strife is that merits such a reward (it seemed to me the Lord took pity on those who live in the world), that I should not think He had forgotten me, that He would never abandon me, but that it was necessary I do what I could. The Lord told me this with comforting compassion. . . .'" (TA)

# ABOUT THE AUTHOR

Craig Turner is a journalist who covered Capitol Hill for a Washington, D.C. news organization during the 1980s. Since then he has also been a writer of magazine and newspaper articles on a variety of issues, including financial matters, cultural issues and religion. He lives in Burke, Virginia, with his wife and three rowdy boys.

 TAN·BOOKS

TAN Books was founded in 1967 to preserve the spiritual, intellectual and liturgical traditions of the Catholic Church. At a critical moment in history TAN kept alive the great classics of the Faith and drew many to the Church. In 2008 TAN was acquired by Saint Benedict Press. Today TAN continues its mission to a new generation of readers.

From its earliest days TAN has published a range of booklets that teach and defend the Faith. Through partnerships with organizations, apostolates, and mission-minded individuals, well over 10 million TAN booklets have been distributed.

More recently, TAN has expanded its publishing with the launch of Catholic calendars and daily planners—as well as Bibles, fiction, and multimedia products through its sister imprints Catholic Courses (CatholicCourses.com) and Saint Benedict Press (SaintBenedictPress.com).

Today TAN publishes over 500 titles in the areas of theology, prayer, devotions, doctrine, Church history, and the lives of the saints. TAN books are published in multiple languages and found throughout the world in schools, parishes, bookstores and homes.

# TAN·CLASSICS

*A collection of the finest literature in the Catholic tradition.*

978-0-89555-227-3

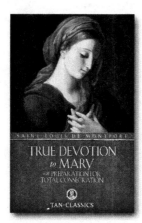

978-0-89555-154-2

978-0-89555-155-9

Our TAN Classics collection is a well-balanced sampling of the finest literature in the Catholic tradition.

978-0-89555-230-3

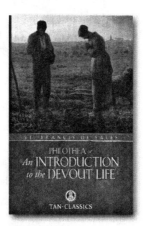

978-0-89555-228-0

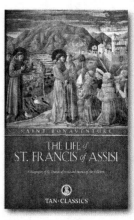

978-0-89555-151-1

TAN·BOOKS

978-0-89555-153-5          978-0-89555-149-8          978-0-89555-199-3

The collection includes distinguished spiritual works of the saints, philosophical treatises and famous biographies.

978-0-89555-226-6          978-0-89555-152-8          978-0-89555-225-9

Visit us at TANBooks.com

*Spread the Faith with . . .*

# TAN·BOOKS

*A Division of Saint Benedict Press, LLC*

---

TAN books are powerful tools for evangelization. They lift the mind to God and change lives. Millions of readers have found in TAN books and booklets an effective way to teach and defend the Faith, soften hearts, and grow in prayer and holiness of life.

Throughout history the faithful have distributed Catholic literature and sacramentals to save souls. St. Francis de Sales passed out his own pamphlets to win back those who had abandoned the Faith. Countless others have distributed the Miraculous Medal to prompt conversions and inspire deeper devotion to God. Our customers use TAN books in that same spirit.

If you have been helped by this or another TAN title, share it with others. Become a TAN Missionary and share our life changing books and booklets with your family, friends and community. We'll help by providing special discounts for books and booklets purchased in quantity for purposes of evangelization. Write or call us for additional details.

**TAN Books**
**Attn: TAN Missionaries Department**
**PO Box 410487**
**Charlotte, NC 28241**


**Toll-free (800) 437-5876**
**missionaries@TANBooks.com**